SOCIOLOGY AND SOCIAL WELFARE SERIES

edited by Paul Halmos

Central Ideas in Sociology

IN THE SAME SERIES

Social Science and Social Purpose
T. S. Simey

Exercises in Social Science
J. Liggett and R. Cochrane

Industrial Democracy
Paul Blumberg

Reader in Social Administration
ed. by A. V. S. Lochhead

Without a Wedding-Ring: Casework with
Unmarried Parents
Jean Pochin

The Personal Service Society
Paul Halmos

Media Sociology
ed. Jeremy Tunstall

The Higher Civil Service in Britain
Richard Chapman

Advances in Social Research
ed. Raymond Cochrane

Homo Religiosus: Sociological problems in
the Study of Religion
Robert Towler

The Structure of Socialist Society
András Hegedüs

BY THE SAME AUTHOR

The Sociology of Grass Roots Politics
(*published by Macmillan*)

Central Ideas in Sociology

AN INTRODUCTION

DAVID BERRY

Lecturer in Sociology,
University College, Cardiff

CONSTABLE
LONDON

3or

14125

First published in Great Britain 1974
by Constable and Company Limited
10 Orange Street London WC2H 7EG
Copyright © 1974 by David Berry

Hardback ISBN 0 09 458180 0
Paperback ISBN 0 09 459820 7

Reprinted 1978

FOR RUTH

Set in Monotype Fournier
Printed in Great Britain by
Redwood Burn Limited
Trowbridge & Esher

Preface

Students of sociology frequently learn about different aspects of sociology – concepts, theories, schools of thought – in a rather atomistic fashion, so that their knowledge of sociology tends to consist of unrelated pieces and segments. I hope that this book will help the student to develop an overall perspective within which his pieces of knowledge can be placed. I have tried to present central theoretical issues in sociology in some depth whilst maintaining readability and intelligibility for those without previous acquaintance with sociological theory.

A book of this length can hardly present a comprehensive introduction to sociological theory, and the table of contents will indicate to the experienced eye that this has not been attempted. As a teacher of sociology, I have never favoured lengthy or comprehensive textbooks, but have preferred students to read widely rather than depend heavily upon a single textbook. There are some fundamental concepts, such as social structure, social change, social organisation and groups, to which I have devoted little attention directly because it seems to me that each of them virtually encompasses the whole of sociology. All sociology is about groups, all sociology is about social structure and social change, and all sociology is about social organisation. The detailed discussion of such concepts here would not, I think, have been particularly helpful. Other concepts are omitted, such as those of social movement, because they refer to a too limited, rather than too extensive, level of generality.

Ultimately, however, the selection of concepts chosen represents my own personal approach to sociology: they do, in my view, represent central themes in sociology today. In that this book presents my own personal view of sociology, it follows that there is much that other sociologists might take issue with. It seemed to me that a more interesting and in the end more useful book might emerge from this approach than from merely reflecting orthodoxies and avoiding controversies. It

5

is not my intention to provide the student with a ready-made socio-logical perspective, but rather to stimulate his imagination so that he may develop his own.

I am indebted to Paul Halmos for encouraging me to write this book and for valuable advice in its preparation. A special debt is also owed to Martin Albrow for his most valuable critical comments. I would also like to thank Geoffrey Mungham, Derrick Carter and Anne Murcott for kindly reading and commenting on draft versions, and Mrs E. M. Nott and Mrs Jane Doran for typing the manuscript.

David Berry
University College, Cardiff   May 1974

Contents

7

8 *Contents*

1. The Perspectives of Sociology

Sociology is perhaps best defined in terms of its perspective on social reality rather than by attempting to carve out a chunk of social reality for its subject matter. The sociologist's construction of social reality depends upon his sociological perspective.

A perspective is a point of view, a particular way of looking at things and organising them so that they become meaningful and intelligible to us. The same events may appear entirely different in meaning to two people who view them from different perspectives. We may have noticed from newspaper reports of court cases that the accounts given – as in the case of a disturbance at a football ground – by the police, witnesses and defendants are quite incompatible. The court is expected to determine what really happened, and to find out who is mistaken or lying. Now the parties in the case may deliberately present a version of the events which is quite different from what they know to have really happened, as in the case of the policeman who has 'planted' a weapon on the defendant, or of the defendant who pretends that he was elsewhere than at the scene of the crime. But it is quite possible for all parties to be telling the 'truth', to be reporting what they saw to have happened, and for the different versions to be still incompatible. This may occur because the different parties at the incident – football fans and policemen – view the situation from different perspectives. Because the policeman's perspective is seen as more authoritative, the courts usually prefer his version of the events. If we see a group of people getting off a motor coach and we are told that they are a party from a social club they may appear to us to be quite different from how the same people would appear had we been told that they were a party of mental patients allowed out for the day. Because in each case we would be viewing them from different perspectives, the visual cues to which we would respond and the ones which we would not notice would be different in each case.

All perspectives are partial and incomplete. A total picture of the situation, taking into account every point of view and every aspect of social reality, is never really possible, because even if we did take into account every point of view that we were aware of, we could never be sure that there were not other points of view which had escaped our notice. Neither can we escape from the problem by saying that we are going to ignore all the various different points of view and simply look at the facts 'as they really are'. Perhaps it would be nice if as sociologists we could climb to the observatory of our academic ivory tower, casting off our social involvements and all the common-sense everyday theories and points of view on the way, and observe society as it really is. The trouble is that were we to carry out this unlikely exercise, we would not be able to observe anything that we could recognise or interpret: the social order would be quite meaningless, in fact there would be no order to observe; we would only be confronted by chaotic and unintelligible stimuli. The sociologist, and for that matter any other member of society, requires a perspective, a frame of reference for ordering the social world and rendering it meaningful and intelligible to him.

It is probably more appropriate to see sociology as based on a set of interrelated perspectives, rather than from a single unified perspective, because sociologists do not share a unified view of the social world. In this chapter, four perspectives are distinguished, perspectives which should be seen to complement each other rather than offer a set of alternative views of social reality. I have said that every member of society, sociologist or not, needs some perspective for the ordering of social reality. The sociologist's perspective should not be seen as an alternative to the everyday, man-in-the-street's conception of social reality, but rather as a perspective that encompasses and builds upon everyday, common-sense perspectives. The course of events in the social world is to a large extent influenced by the meanings and interpretations that people have of events, and it is important that the sociologist should take these meanings into account in the construction of his theories. In presenting the four sociological perspectives, therefore, I have tried to show how they relate to everyday conceptions of the social world.

SOCIETY

The magistrate informs the hapless prisoner that his offence is an outrage against society, that society will not tolerate his behaviour. The disillusioned middle-class youth wants to opt out, and do his own thing, and so becomes a hippie, just as, more rarely, the middle-aged *rentier* chooses to opt out by retreating to a cottage in the wilds of the north-west Highlands of Scotland. For our prisoner, hippie, and *rentier*, society is demanding, society is restraining, society is oppressive. The notion of 'opting out' implies that the choice for the individual is between accepting his position in society as it is laid out for him, or rejecting it. There are the parts that society has destined him to play: husband, bank clerk, suburban commuter; the script is more or less complete, and the stage directions leave little room for manoeuvre; the only alternative to taking the role laid out for him is to opt out. A less extreme view, but one that shares a similar conception of society, is held by those who are preoccupied with conformity. According to one group of American sociologists,[1] twentieth-century American society is characterised by an increase in pressures to conformity, an increasing tendency of people to wish to be, above all, like everyone else. At the same time, one can detect an increasing tendency among groups of younger people to react against and denigrate conformity, no doubt partly induced by the popularisation of this American sociological critique of conformity. For these people the conformist is despised rather than emulated, is seen as unreflective, lacking spontaneity and imagination, a plaster-cast from society's mould, a pale shadow of humanity. Both the conformist, anxious lest he should fail to live up to society's requirements, and the critic of conformity share a similar view of social reality. They both see society as a powerful force restraining and suppressing individuality.

In these popular conceptions, society is seen more or less as an impersonal force, influencing, restraining, even determining the behaviour of its members. These notions bear a close resemblance to the sociologist's perspective of society, a perspective which depends largely on the work of the classic French sociologist, Emile Durkheim. For Durkheim, society was an objective reality in its own right, independent of the particular individuals who were its members. We must, he says, 'seek the explanation of social life in the nature of society itself'.[2] Society is 'not a mere sum of individuals. Rather, the system formed by their association represents a specific reality which has its own characteristics.'[3] Uniformities found in behaviour in given societies – that, for example, the English are very adept at forming orderly queues at bus-stops, shops, and cinemas, but are exceptionally undisciplined as pedestrians crossing roads – are to be seen as a product of the society, and not in terms of any inherent characteristics of the individual members. Uniformities in individual behaviour are to be seen as socially determined, and such uniformities may be very far-reaching. This may be illustrated by considering the range of behaviours and attitudes of the individual that may be predicted simply on the basis of his occupation and the type of secondary school he attended. The ex-public school stockbroker is likely to wear certain kinds of clothes, varied appropriately according to the social occasion, and to live in a certain type of house in a certain type of area – a large detached house in either a very leafy suburb or an apparently rustic village. The garden is likely to be formal, with large expanses of grass, shrubs and roses, but without any striking patches of bright colour. We could even make some fairly reliable predictions about the décor and furnishings of the house: no brightly patterned wallpapers, or contrastingly coloured imitation leather three-piece suites will be found here. He will probably be Conservative in his politics and high Anglican in his religion. His attitudes to crime will be relatively tough, and he will believe that people are basically wicked and must be controlled and restrained by society. Such a picture is, of course, a stereotype, not perhaps very different from that produced in our everyday social theories, though the sociologist's stereotype is based on the systematic collection of evidence of observed uniformities, whereas the everyday stereotype may be a product of unsubstantiated popular beliefs. For the sociologist, too, the characteristics of our stockbroker are not things that are inherent in the nature of stockbrokers, but a result of the stockbroker being placed in a particular slot in society. The role is cast for him by society – not merely his activities directly related to his work, but a whole range of other activities, his family life, his leisure, which fit in with what is expected of stockbrokers.

The perspective of society is a determinist, anti-individualistic perspective. It is open to the objection that it tends to treat society as some sort of mystical force, controlling individuals as the puppeteer controls his puppets. Against this objection, however, it may be said that while society can be no more than the social association of its members, it is nevertheless *experienced* as an independent, objective reality by its members. Our hippie and others who wish to opt out experience society as a determining, restraining force upon their activities. Society as an external, constraining force is very real to them. They are, of course, a small minority, as are those who view with dismay the conformity all around them, and probably even those who are anxious lest they should fail to conform. For most people most of the time, society is not experienced as constraining or repressive; it is not noticed at all. We do what we want to do, we make our choices, we behave as ourselves, but to the sociologist society is no less in evidence. It is rather that we willingly fit into the roles that society has set out for us, or, put more cynically, that we are willing lambs to the slaughter. The teenager listens to the latest pop tunes and follows the latest fashions because he likes them; and not because other teenagers do the same; the junior business executive plants neat rows of miniature conifers along the drive of his new suburban house because he likes them, and not because other junior business executives moving into similar houses do the same. From the perspective of society, our freely made choices are themselves socially determined: we have learned to want to play the part that is laid out for us. The determinism of the sociologist's perspective of society is much more all-encompassing than the everyday conception of those who want to opt out. The hippie makes his choice between fitting into society or opting out: but for the sociologist, his choice of opting out may be more apparent than real: the very choice will be seen very much as a product of his particular set of circumstances, and opting out itself rather as exchanging one set of social constraints for another. In their dress and style of life hippies would appear to be as much subject to the constraints of their social group as anyone else. From the perspective of society even those who recognise and react against social conformity are still determined in their actions by society.

Students may find the sociologist's determinist perspective of society somewhat depressing. Most people like to believe that they do exercise free choice in at least some areas of their behaviour. The student may become resigned to the view that for much of his time he is in fact acting out the role that is set for him, but (he will protest) the sociologist cannot have everything. The sociologist cannot have the student's spontaneity, individuality, humanity; he is more than the sociologist's determinist image of him. Some sociologists have not been unsympathetic to such a cry of protest, among them Ralf Dahrendorf:

> However we turn and twist *homo sociologicus*, he will never be the particular person who is our friend, colleague, father or brother. *Homo sociologicus* can neither love nor hate, laugh nor cry. He remains a pale, incomplete, strange, artificial man.[4]

Other sociologists are less responsive. Erving Goffman writes:

> There is a vulgar tendency in social thought to divide the conduct
> of the individual into a profane and sacred part. . . . The profane
> part is attributed to the obligatory world of social roles; it is formal,
> stiff and dead; it is exacted by society. The sacred part has to do
> with 'personal' matters and 'personal' relationships – with what the
> individual is 'really' like underneath it all when he relaxes and
> breaks through to those in his presence. It is here, in this personal
> capacity, that an individual can be warm, spontaneous, and touched
> by humour. It is here, regardless of his social role, that an individual
> can show 'what kind of guy he is'. And so it is, that in showing
> that a given piece of conduct is part of the obligations and trappings
> of a role, one shifts it from the sacred category to the profane, from
> the fat and living to the thin and dead. Sociologists *qua* sociologists
> are allowed to have the profane part; sociologists *qua* persons,
> along with other persons, retain the sacred for their friends, their
> wives and themselves.[5]

In his sociology, Goffman is not content with the profane; the sacred –
warmth, spontaneity, humour and individuality – are also part of his
sociological man, grist for the sociological mill and thus to be seen in
the context of social influences. Is human spontaneity therefore not to
be spared from the grasp of the deterministic vision of the sociologist?
The student may see the student party as an example of human spontaneity beyond the territory of the sociologist. Here, at least, people
cast off restraints, let their hair down, are uninhibited and truly themselves. Or so it may seem. But if we look closer, the spontaneity
exhibited may appear to show certain uniformities, and even at the
wildest parties, rules may be discerned as to types of spontaneity which
are permitted and those types which are not. To let one's hair down in
the appropriate manner may be the requirement of the evening, and
not to do this may incur severe social disapproval. The professor may
be as much put out by students who act towards him at a party as they
would at a seminar as by those who act towards him in a seminar as
they would at a party!

Yet it would be a mistake to dismiss Dahrendorf's plea to limit the
sociologist in his scope too lightly. Dahrendorf is concerned with the
moral consequences of sociological knowledge, the effects upon
society of the acceptance of a socially determined conception of man.
It is, he remarks, 'only a step from seeing man as a mere role player to

the alienated world of *1984*, where all loving and hating, all dreaming and acting, all individuality beyond the grasp of roles, become a crime against society – society in this sense being sociology hypostatised'.[6] It is indeed the responsibility of the sociologist to be concerned with the moral consequences of his actions – and these actions include his theorising. This important point is taken up in the concluding chapter of this book, but here we are concerned with the validity rather than the ethics of sociological accounts. If our conception of sociological man formed from the deterministic perspective of society seems incomplete, inadequate, less than human, the appropriate course of action is not to place limits upon the sociologist, to preserve the private personality from his analysis, lest he destroy our beliefs in human individuality and foster inhumanity in the world. This would be to detach sociology from the real world of experience, to separate the sociologist as a sociologist from the sociologist as a person. If socio-logical man of our deterministic perspective of society is incomplete and subhuman, then we must extend, not contract, the scope of sociology. In order to understand man in society, we must inject humanity into our sociology. The perspective of society must be supplemented by other perspectives if the sociologist is to understand human action. First, however, we must consider a perspective which not only fails to answer the problem posed here, but reinforces the apparent determinism and anti-individuality of sociology. This per-spective, which has often been dominant in the work of twentieth-century sociologists is the perspective of the social system.

THE SOCIAL SYSTEM

This perspective is a derivative and extension of the perspective of 'society' rather than a distinctly separate perspective. While the similarities between the two will emerge clearly from the discussion, the distinctive contribution of the 'systems' perspective merits it being treated separately here.

It may be helpful to begin, as with the perspective of society, by relating the 'system' perspective to everyday lay social theories. The everyday conception of 'the system' may, in the same way as the every-day conception of society, reflect attitudes of fatalism and powerless-ness, the idea that the individual is at the mercy of forces beyond his control. 'You can't buck the system' is a saying that encapsulates this attitude. In everyday social theories, the notions of 'society' and 'the system' may be almost synonymous, but this is not always so. Firstly, while 'the system' may refer to the system of society, and the impersonal power of the system over the individual, it may refer to very specific and limited sectors of the individual's life experience – his work situation, for example. For the middle-class business executive oriented to 'getting ahead' it is 'the system' that enslaves him to the unsavoury aspects of the 'rat race'. For the university lecturer, it is 'the system' that demands his involvement in the more petty and sordid aspects of academic politics, and the system that produces professors who seem to be authoritarian and obsessed with power, until he becomes one himself. For the radical Christian, it is the system that produces clergymen who do not believe in God. For the idealistic political activist, it is the system that places self-seeking careerists in high places. 'The system' may serve as an apology for indulging in admittedly immoral behaviour, a justification for apparent irrationalities, or an explanation of the impossibility of bringing about changes. What is distinctive about the conception is that it refers to the way things are organised. If the concept is used to refer to a distinctive organisation – the church, the university, the industrial enterprise – it may be recognised that it was once consciously constructed. However, it is seen to generate its own momentum, generate its own mechanisms for perpetuating itself, and its own devices for ensuring that the individuals associated with it serve its own requirements. 'The system' is anonymous, and cannot be identified with specific individuals. In its everyday conception it may appear, as 'society' may appear, as some sort of mystical entity.

The sociologist's perspective of the social system has been developed to a large extent by borrowing from the perspectives of the natural sciences, originally from biology and mechanics, more recently from cybernetics. It does, however, share some of the characteristics of the everyday conception of the 'system'. It refers to the way social life is ordered and organised. It may refer to large-scale society, to a sector of society – the educational sector, perhaps – or to a small group – the family, perhaps, as a social system. Through the perspective of the social system, social life is viewed as ordered in such a way that every aspect of social life is intricately, even if very indirectly, related to every other aspect. Changes and developments in one sphere of social activity are seen to generate changes and developments, or reactions, in other spheres. Changes in the economic and industrial sphere, or subsystem of the social system of society, could be considered in terms of their implications for the political sphere, or subsystem. We might consider the development of the political system of parliamentary democracy in Britain as related to the development of industrial capitalism, or the development of the educational system as related to the occupational system. The social system perspective is a determinist perspective: change in any element of the system is determined by the other elements, and at the same time each element is in part a determinant of all the other elements. The determinism of the system perspective is attractive to sociologists because it provides the possibility of prediction. If we can describe the way in which different aspects of social life are related to each other as a social system, then we may be able to predict the consequences of events in one sphere of social life for other spheres. Conversely, it has been said that if sociologists do not accept the notion of some sort of balanced relationship between the different aspects of social life, then it is not possible to predict the consequences of different events.[7] If, for example, educational institutions cannot be related in a systematic way to other social institutions, then, it would be argued, it would not be possible to predict the broad social consequences of educational changes, nor of the consequences of other social changes for the educational system. Its association with prediction is probably one of the most important contributions of the social system perspective.

There are two basic ways in which the different elements of the social system may be seen to be acting upon each other. The first is where a given change in one sphere produces reactions in other spheres with the result that the system maintains itself in a given state: a given change generates reactions so that the equilibrium, or the *status quo ante*, is restored. For example, economic grievances may give rise to industrial unrest, strikes and demonstrations, thus threatening the given social order. Agencies of social control then react to this: the police are strengthened, troops may be sent in, and leaders are arrested and given exemplary punishments. Possibly, too, the authorities meet some of the most pressing (that is from the point of view of maintaining social order) economic grievances; the initial unrest is then controlled or suppressed. So a change in one element of the system is met by a reaction in other parts, the consequence of which is to restore the balance of the system, the *status quo*. The second way in which elements in the social system interact is whereby a given change in one sphere produces effects in other spheres, the overall consequence of which is to produce yet further changes and magnify the initial change in the system. In the hypothetical example given, the reaction of the agencies of social control to the initial industrial unrest may lead to something very different from a restoration of order and a return to the *status quo*. Confrontation with soldiers and exemplary punishment of leaders – seen by followers as martyrdom – may transform the situation from a protest about wages and conditions of work into a full-scale revolutionary movement bent on overthrowing the given social order. The notion that the relationship between elements of the social system is such that changes and developments tend to be amplified rather than reduced has been extensively employed by sociologists studying deviance.[8] Thus, the apprehension of the juvenile offender by the police, his court appearance, and his Borstal sentence may be more likely to confirm him in a criminal career than to restore him to the paths of 'good citizenship'. He has been publicly labelled as a criminal, and as such will find many of the paths to 'good citizenship' closed to him on the completion of his sentence. Moreover, from his stay in a penal institution, he will probably have gained, if little else, an apprenticeship in the basic skills required for a criminal career.

Sociologists employing the social system approach have tended to emphasise the mechanisms whereby the social system maintains itself in a given state, mechanisms whereby the equilibrium, and thus the *status quo*, is maintained. Such an emphasis, focusing upon the conditions for the maintenance of a given social order, is conservative. Other conservative tendencies, too, can be discerned within the systems perspective. If society is conceived as a social system, then whatever changes occur in society, these are unlikely to be seen as equivalent to changes in the basic principles and structure of the system model. The principles by which the elements of the system are related to each other are fixed and unchanging. Indeed, if this were not the case, the system model would be unable to cope with major social changes. If the principles and basic structure of the system model no longer seem applicable to a society after a revolution, then the sociologist would have to discard his system model and start afresh. If the system model is not to be limited in its relevance to a particular society with a particular social structure, but is to be of general and universal applicability, then it must be conceived in terms of at least some fixed and enduring principles. The trouble is that the fixed structure and principles of the model become identified with the particular social order of a particular society, with the resulting tendency for that social order to be regarded as fixed and unchangeable in its basic structure. Thus, there is a tendency for some political sociologists to regard the prevailing order of parliamentary democracy in certain Western societies as enduring and unchangeable in its basic structure: parties may rise or fall and electoral procedures may be modified, but the principle of government elected as a result of competition for the popular vote between two or more parties is assumed to be an unchanging and unchangeable feature of the structure of the system.

It could be argued that the conservative tendencies of sociologists in their application of the system perspective are not inherent in the perspective, but derive from the particular ways in which it is applied, though this is a matter of debate. There can be little doubt, however, about the anti-individualism inherent in the systems perspective. From the perspective of society, the individual appears as little more than a puppet, fitting into the mould or slot that society has provided for him. This may be soulless enough, but from the systems perspective the individual as a person seems to be in danger of disappearing from view altogether. For the components of the system are not individual people: they are subsystems; educational, political, economic, religious and other subsystems. Nor are the components of these subsystems individual people, but further system components, usually depicted according to their functions in the system. Of course, the working of the system depends upon the activities of individuals, but there is no specific place for the individual in the system model. When sociologists employing the system perspective discuss needs, they are not usually talking about human needs, but about the needs of the system – the requirements that must be met if the system is to maintain itself. It is primarily the system that has goals to be attained, not the individual. It may be stated that the system must satisfy certain minimum needs of individuals, but the reason for this requirement is to ensure that individuals adapt to the system and fulfil the tasks that the system requires of them. The farmer must feed his turkeys if they are to be fat enough to kill for Christmas. The social system perspective does not lead the sociologist to ask whether in fact the needs of individuals might be incompatible with the needs of the system. Sometimes, it is simply assumed that the needs of the system and the needs of individuals are complementary, which is not unlike the homily of the businessman that what is good for industry is good for the people. Fundamentally, the social system perspective is concerned with individual needs only in so far as they impinge upon system needs. From its anti-individualistic standpoint, the approach otherwise ignores the individual. The chief value of the system perspective is that it enables us to develop a framework whereby we may show how diverse aspects of social life are interrelated. But for a human conception of socio-logical man we must look to other perspectives.

POWER AND CONFLICT

The popular, everyday conception of 'the system' may serve as a point of departure for the discussion of this third perspective. Those for whom 'the system' is the basis for feelings of impotence, fatalism and powerlessness, though not those for whom 'the system' provides a justification for otherwise immoral actions, may reflect that it is not altogether impersonal: the system seems to favour some people at the expense of others. Furthermore, it may seem that it serves the interests of the favoured to maintain the system. Perhaps the reason for the continuance of the system is more to do with the power of these people, rather than with any impersonal mechanisms. Such a view sees the procedures and workings of social life as much in terms of power and conflict as in terms of a notion of 'system'. Perhaps the simplest every-day power and conflict theory of society is that characteristic of certain sections of the British working class. In this view, it is not so much 'society' that makes demands upon, restrains, and controls me as an individual: 'society' in fact consists of 'them' and 'us', and it is 'they' who make demands upon and exercise control over 'us'; 'they' are the authorities and the people who decide things. It may be seen to be because 'they' know what is best, and it is not for the likes of 'us' to interfere (an attitude of deference), or more simply because 'they' have power and 'we' don't.

The working-class view of the world as a division between 'them' and 'us' has been well described by Richard Hoggart:

> 'Them' is a composite dramatic figure, the chief character in modern urban forms of the rural peasant–big-house relationships. The world of 'Them' is the world of the bosses, whether those bosses are private individuals, or as is increasingly the case today, public officials. 'Them' may be, as occasion requires, anyone from the classes outside other than the few individuals from those classes whom working people know as individuals. . . .

> 'They' are 'the people at the top', 'the higher-ups', the people who give you your dole, call you up, tell you to go to war, fine you, made you split the family in the thirties to avoid a reduction in the Means Test allowance, 'get yer in the end', 'aren't really to be

trusted', 'Talk posh', 'are all twisters really', 'Never tell yer owt' (e.g. about a relative in hospital), 'clap yer in clink', 'will do y' down if they can', 'summons yer', 'are all in a click' (clique) 'together', 'treat y' like muck'.[9]

Our third sociological perspective, then, is the perspective of power and conflict. The first thing to be said about it is that it provides an immediate counterweight to the impersonality of the 'society' and 'system' perspectives. If 'society' demands conformity, if the 'system' has needs, then from our third perspective we must ask who demands conformity of whom, who sets out the roles we have to play, and whose needs are the needs of the system or society? The impersonal force of 'society' now emerges as dependent on the relative power of different social groups in society. It is perhaps possible to conceive of a society in which power is equally diffused throughout the population, but it is probable that such a society has never actually existed. The power and conflict perspective places its initial focus on the distribution of power in society, and the given social order is seen to be dependent on the location of power. The dominant rules which prescribe and determine our position and behaviour in social life are seen to reflect the interests of the powerful groups in society. It is not that the social order is consciously planned and constructed by a dominant group in some sort of conspiratorial manner, but that the powerful – by virtue of their power – are in an advantageous position to strengthen and reinforce these rules which serve their interests, and to change those that do not.

Thus, it was in the interests of early nineteenth-century industrialists in England to reinforce the traditional value of the subservience of the lower orders in society to their superiors, but to reject the traditional aristocratic values of paternal responsibility for the welfare of the lower orders. The requirements of their enterprises demanded both a subservient working class and an economic and social doctrine of *laissez-faire*.[10] The apprenticeship clauses of the Elizabethan Statute of Artificers, which enforced apprenticeships and thereby protected the wages of artisans in certain trades, were repealed in 1814, and even half a century previously an assize judge had refused to enforce it because it might be a restriction on trade.[11] The Poor Law Amendment Act of 1834, in instituting the punitive workhouses and abolishing or severely restricting any relief outside the workhouses, rendered the Poor Laws more compatible with the economic doctrine of *laissez-faire*. These changes were in the interests of industrialists, and can be explained in terms of the increasing power of industrialists in nineteenth-century England.

This is not to suggest that powerful groups cynically calculate the moral doctrines that will serve their material interests and devise and promote them accordingly, though this may sometimes happen. There is evidence that many ordinary people in Britain today doubt the sincerity of politicians in expressing the political principles by which they justify their power.[12] It is more usually the case that people tend to hold beliefs which are in accordance with their interests and social circumstances. It is not, perhaps, too difficult for the rich man to believe that he is rich because he is virtuous, and that people are poor because they are wicked, or, in the more enlightened times of today, 'inadequate'. The alternatives may be rather uncomfortable.

The restraints of society upon the individual, then, are to be seen in terms of the distribution of power in society. To return to nineteenth-century England, the dominance of offences against property in the penal code, many of them capital offences, can be seen to reflect the dominant power of the propertied classes. In the words of E. P. Thompson, 'The greatest offence against property was to have none'.[13] Even today the majority of British prison inmates are offenders against the laws of property.

Sometimes the distribution of power in society is quite clearcut and distinctive, so that it is possible to distinguish a dominant or ruling class and a subordinate class or classes. The power perspective is consistent with a view of society composed of social classes distinguished in terms of power, classes which are actually or potentially in conflict with one another: the classic Marxist conception of capitalist society is such a view, though it is by no means the only one.*

The different distribution of power between different social groups, or classes, is associated with potential or actual conflict between these groups. This follows from the proposition that unless power is equally distributed, the exercise of power by the more powerful groups is always, to a greater or lesser extent, at the expense of the less powerful.† In simple terms, powerful groups, by virtue of their power, are in a much stronger position to defend their interests and to ensure that the social order reflects their interests. In practice, things never

---

* The relationship between power and social classes is discussed in Chapter 6.

† As will be seen in Chapter 6 (pp. 138–9), not all conceptions of power are consistent with this proposition.

appear to be quite like this. Political authorities when confronted with opposition, rarely answer it by saying, in effect, that they are the masters, the opposition is powerless, and therefore the masters decide, though from an objective viewpoint the failure of opposition may be seen in terms of its lack of power. Thus, a local housing authority confronted with opposition to its urban programme from a working-class community adversely affected by this programme may ignore the opposition ostensibly because it is produced by the agitation of a few troublemakers, is 'politically motivated', sentimental or irrational and not in the true interests of the people who do not know what is best for them anyway. However, the failure of the opposition may be due more to its lack of power in the face of the power of the local authority than to its lack of rational argument. In an impoverished working-class community of Cardiff a local residents' association, of which the author was secretary, in the course of a twelve-month campaign to change urban renewal plans affecting its members, failed to persuade the local authority to consider its case, or even to recognise its existence by replying to its letters. This was despite overwhelming evidence of popular support, the support of the local M.P., extensive and sympathetic coverage by the local press, and the election of a local councillor during the period whose campaign was based solely on the case of the residents' association. But the ruling group on the council had such a large majority that it was virtually immune from defeat through electoral unpopularity,* and so the association, appealing only to 'public opinion', was unable to mount any effective challenge.[14]

However, powerful groups should not necessarily be regarded as cynical: they may well believe that their actions are right and in accordance with their moral principles. More generally, their actions will be consistent with their view of the social world. But the sociologist sees that this view is a product of their particular social situation; a situation of power and privilege. Underprivileged and powerless groups, by virtue of their situation, are always likely to generate views of the social world which are at odds with those of the rich and powerful. The views of the powerful, however, are likely to be dominant because, by virtue of their power, they are in advantageous positions to persuade others to accept. In the words of Marx and Engels, 'the

---

* Two subsequent years of clear electoral defeat still left this party in control. This was possible because only one-third of the councillors were re-elected each year, and because the ruling group still held all the aldermanic seats.

ideas of the ruling class are in every epoch the ruling ideas'.[15] Thus, the child at Sunday School in the nineteenth century, impoverished and stunted by the most atrocious conditions of child labour, might learn the virtues of duty, obedience and industry, how it was wicked to be discontented, that if he was a good boy he would be rewarded in heaven, but would otherwise be burned in hell.[16] Today, opinions of the 'experts' are probably more persuasive than religious terrorism: the expert economic advisers, the expert planners, the expert crimino-logists, who move mostly in the circles of the powerful and privileged, share many of their rewards, and, above all, share their view of the social world.

If, through a dominant influence in organised religion, the mass media, the schools and other means, the more powerful groups in society are able to persuade large sections of the less powerful groups to accept their world view, then the social order is relatively har-monious, conflict is limited. Social conflict is, however, suppressed rather than removed, because in so far as the social situation of the powerless and underprivileged differs from that of the powerful and the privileged, they are in their social relations likely to develop theories and views of the world which challenge the existing power structure. The development of close-knit working-class communities, with their members sharing the same social, economic and industrial experiences, may generate social solidarity and political radicalism. Nowhere in Britain is perhaps this more evident than in the mining valleys of South Wales.

The perspective of power and conflict is more humanistic than those of 'society' and 'the social system'. The process and ordering of social life no longer appears as just the consequence of the impersonal 'forces of society' and the impersonal, anonymous mechanisms of the 'social system', but as the product of human actions: the actions of the powerful who seek to preserve the *status quo*, and of the powerless who seek to challenge it. It is thus less deterministic. It is humanistic in that it focuses attention upon individual needs rather than needs of 'society'. Whose needs, we are forced to ask, does society serve? It is not, however, to be seen as an alternative to the perspectives of 'society' and the 'social system', but as a necessary complement to these perspectives. As we have seen, the world view of the powerful is a product of their social situation, and is thus socially determined. The member of the working-class community is not merely restrained and controlled by the social organisation of the powerful: his social association in the working-class community also imposes its restraints, demands and requirements, and in the close-knit community these may well be experienced as more important than those of 'them'. The restraints of 'society' upon the individual are much more than the requirements of a ruling class. The development of conflicts may be dependent upon human actions, but the outcomes of these actions may be very different from their intended consequences. The unintended consequences of intended actions may be seen to be dependent upon the complex interrelationship between different aspects of social life. The generation of conflict and its containment may be seen as a product of the interrelationship of these different aspects of social life: it may be examined in terms of the processes of society as a social system. Thus the judge, intending to punish and thereby reform the prisoner, may publicly brand him as a 'menace to society', and so do his part to ensure he remains so. The agencies of social control, in attempting to suppress industrial unrest, may do their part in generating a revolutionary movement. Social reformers may use methods to achieve their ends which may be seen by the uncommitted as extremist, and thus a movement for reaction is generated.

From the perspective of power and conflict, society appears as potentially conflicting groups and classes whose relative positions depend on the distribution of power. Though the perspective may draw attention to individual, as opposed to 'societal' or 'system' needs, it is the group, and above all the class, not the individual that is central. Sociological man is beginning to bear some resemblance to what we know to be human, but it would still seem to be the case that sociology is the study of groups and unconcerned with the individual. For a genuinely humanistic sociology, a fourth perspective must be added: what we may term the individualistic or phenomenological perspective; phenomenological because it focuses on the nature of reality as it is experienced by the individual.

THE INDIVIDUALISTIC PERSPECTIVE

'Society', the 'system', social classes, are all very large-scale concepts. Whatever the failings of the perspectives outlined above, it may seem they cannot be accused of being narrow or trivial. With such broad perspectives on the nature of society and its organisation, the sociologist, it may seem, is equipped and ready to confront and contribute to the major social issues of our time. In contrast, the individualistic perspective is very much concerned with the seemingly trivial, the mundane, ordinary, everyday social world. The sociologist emphasising this perspective may, to give some actual examples, spend his time studying the behaviour of children on a merry-go-round, the intricacies of social relationships in a small hotel, or even a family discussion on the purchase of a pair of shoes. Surely such activities are trivial, symptomatic of sociologists who are unconcerned with the major social issues, concerned only with their little world of social research? It is too easy to jump to this conclusion. I have already argued that a genuine academic sociology cannot be detached from the real world of experience. The sociologist has a responsibility for the consequences of his activities, and today many sociologists, including the author, recognise the responsibility of sociologists for their research to be socially relevant. A cursory scanning of sociological journals may well confirm the view that at least some of the activities of sociologists are trivial and socially irrelevant: the focus on the esoteric and bizarre, and the obscure refinements of the obscure classifications of obscure little theories may sometimes merit such a description. But we must be wary of applying the label of trivia unreflectingly. It may be that sociologists' activities are simply not in accordance with accepted, dominant definitions of what is important and what they ought to be doing according to the established 'authorities'.

Before we dismiss the attention of sociology to the mundane, ordinary, and seemingly trivial aspects of everyday life, it might be reflected that for most people a very large part of social life is very ordinary and mundane. Perhaps some of the attraction of the sociology of the esoteric, the bizarre, the out-of-the-ordinary is the escape from the mundane, ordinary and perhaps rather dull social world. Even plays films and television serials that purport to deal with routine everyday life rarely, in fact, do anything of the kind. To hold the interest of their audiences, they must focus on the unexpected, the extraordinary, the exceptions in the routine of everyday life. To ignore the mundane, the ordinary, then, is to ignore a large part of social life. Such an approach might be justified on the grounds that such activities are not socially significant, important or relevant. So, for the sociologist committed to the construction of a better society, there are more important things to do than to look at family discussions concerning shopping expeditions and the behaviour of children at fairgrounds. But can we be sure that routine, everyday, commonplace activities have nothing to do with major social issues? Can we be sure that the routine, everyday activities of policemen have nothing to do with the problem of delinquency, that the routine, everyday activities of social workers and welfare agencies are irrelevant to the study of poverty and 'problem' families, that the routine, everyday activities of ordinary members of political parties have nothing to do with the political structure and problems of democracy?

In terms of the 'individualistic' perspective, we examine the structure of society by proceeding from the individual's own personal construction of the social world. This construction includes both an appraisal of one's everyday activities, a view of what is appropriate and decorous behaviour in everyday social situations, together with more macroscopic views of the construction and ordering of society – society ordered into a hierarchy of status according to ability and moral excellence, or perhaps alternatively ordered into the powerful and the powerless. Everyday behaviour must be consistent with the individual's view of his position within the social order, and, ultimately, with his view, and his assumptions about the construction of the social order. This point could be illustrated by considering the case of a person highly committed to a religious view of the world. For such a person, no action, however small and insignificant, can be undertaken other than in accordance with the religious creed. Now it may be apparent that while many religious believers accept the ideal that all their actions should be in accordance with their religious creed, in practice very few will believe that they succeed in living up to it. So their behaviour will not be altogether in accordance with their religious view of the world. The point to be made here is not that people attempt to live up to some ideal code of behaviour, but that their actions are *in fact* consistent with their world view, their construction of the social world, and the view of their position in it. The businessman who goes to church on Sunday but the next day meets a protest at a harsh decision by the rejoinder that he is not running a Sunday School can be seen to be in both instances acting in terms of a consistent world view that assigns appropriate places to religious and business activities.

That there is a consistency between everyday activity and the broader aspects of the structure of society has been appreciated by certain contemporary radical movements in Western societies. Notable among these are the 'alternative' or 'underground' press in Britain, and the Students for a Democratic Society in the United States of America. Their activities have caused offence to conventional views by words and deeds that are regarded as obscene. Such groups try deliberately to shock those who accept traditional standards of decency and decorum, conventional standards of everyday behaviour, because the acceptance of these standards is associated with the acceptance of the given status order, the *status quo*, which the radical seeks to overthrow. If people start to question conventional standards of decency and decorum, so the argument might run, then they may be led to question the social order on which these standards are based. Supporters of the defendants in a recent obscenity trial over the publication of an issue of the underground newspaper *Oz* claimed that the trial was political: in other words, that the publication was seen by the authorities as a threat to the political order rather than merely to moral 'decency'. Now whether such activities as the publication of four-letter words or defecation in university filing cabinets are conducive to the spread of political radicalism is a matter for debate. The point here is that the ordering by the individual of his everyday activities is dependent upon the same world view whereby he sees the ordering of society. The morality of everyday life, decency and decorum, is not separable from the morality of the wider social and political order. The common-sense everyday theories whereby people interpret the social order and their own everyday activities within it may be unreflective, un-examined, dependent upon taken-for-granted, and even unnoticed, assumptions. For the sociologist, the study of the mundane, and of the ordinary in everyday life may reveal the nature of such unnoticed assumptions, and these may turn out to be very relevant to the major features of the structure of society. The social worker's definitions and taken-for-granted assumptions about the ordering of everyday life may play a major part in her decision as to whether a delinquent comes from a 'good' or 'bad' home; and it is the delinquent from a 'bad' home who is more likely to be sent to some form of residential institu-tion and thus be prepared for a criminal career.

Much of the argument of the preceding paragraph depends upon the view that the way in which people interpret their social world is a major determinant of the course of events in the social world. Patterns of juvenile delinquency are not, in this view, to be seen in terms of the operation of the impersonal forces of society and the social system, but in terms of the way in which social workers and those responsible for social control understand and interpret actions and events, and the interpretations of the situation of those who themselves are depicted as the delinquents. It is not so much the attention to the ordinary and mundane, but the focus on the interpretations and meanings of social life for the participants that is the distinctive contribution of the individualistic perspective.

From the perspective of 'society' we obtained a caricature of the individual as a determined and predestined creature assigned to his role prepared for him by society. From the individualistic perspective, however, 'society' itself only exists in so far as it is experienced and understood by individuals. What determines the behaviour of the individual is not so much social influences which directly mould and manipulate him as if he were a puppet, but his perception and interpretation of these influences. The soldier on duty in an area of civil disturbances, even given his rigid training and detailed orders as to how to respond to events, does not in fact simply respond to the events as they happen – the throwing of a stone or a bottle, the appearance of a figure on a roof-top – and according to his orders. He reacts according to his interpretation of the significance of these events. If his reactions cause widespread public protests – as might occur where civilian demonstrators are shot – then a resulting inquiry might be concerned with whether the soldier's interpretation of the events was a proper, reasonable, or correct one. Had the demonstration become a riot? Was the man who was killed about to throw a petrol bomb?

Sociological man no longer seems to be a predetermined puppet: although subject to social influences, he now appears more of a free individual in his personal interpretation of these influences. However, our sociological man does not quite so easily escape from the determinist shackles that the sociological perspective has imposed upon him. For the process whereby the member of society interprets and defines the situation is itself subject to social influences: he will arrive at a definition of the situation that is consistent with his view of the world, which is itself a product of his social circumstances. The way in which the soldier interprets and defines events in the course of a civil disturbance, together with his view of himself in the situation, is a product of his social position and situation, and his view of the social world that he has learnt in the course of his military training. To take a further military example, we may be shocked by reports of military atrocities, of instances where whole populations of villages, men, women, and children, are killed, and it may appear that these instances occur because the soldiers have been corrupted and become mentally unbalanced by the process of warfare. But perhaps such actions can be seen as consequences of interpretations of the situation in which the village population is defined as both hostile and subhuman, the women are seen as the supporters of enemy troops and the children as potential enemy troops. The record of inhumanity, in the twentieth-century world, the record of gas chambers, nuclear destruction, napalm, torture and mass starvation bears witness to the scope of the ability of men to devise interpretations of their situation to justify such abominable actions. In viewing such interpretations not in terms of inherent human wickedness, but in terms of their social circumstances – circumstances which are not inevitable but are themselves a product of men's actions – the sociologist's determinist view might appear as more optimistic than pessimistic.

In focusing on the individual's interpretation and definition of his social situation, we have, in fact, already moved away from the somewhat rigid determinism of the perspectives of 'society' and the 'social system'. The interpretation is produced by the individual, not by society, albeit that social constraints are still operative upon the individual. But from the individualistic perspective, it is not just that the individual acts according to his definition of the situation. In his actions he also seeks to influence the way in which other people interpret and define events. In our everyday social activities we seek to persuade others to accept our interpretation and definition of the situation and our view of our own position in the situation. This is not the same thing as persuading other people to agree with our opinions: it may be said that social intercourse is impossible without some element of shared definition of the situation. If other people do not accept us as fundamentally the sort of people we think we are, then social life is indeed impossible, as it is for those who see themselves as Messiahs or Napoleons, but fail to persuade others to accept their view of themselves and consequently become the inhabitants of mental hospitals. To take less extreme examples, the probation officer seeks to persuade his client that the situation is one in which the client is to be 'helped'. He may be prepared to cope with the client's definition of the situation as one of enforced submission to authority, but would probably be unable to cope if the client defined the situation as one in which the probation officer is to be 'helped'. Sometimes, people fail to convince others of their definition of the situation because they are unable to conceal, or unwittingly reveal, information that is inconsistent with their definition. The consequence may be acute embarrassment, as in the case of the supposedly faithful husband who has failed to remove traces of discrediting make-up before meeting his wife, or the pop singer whose recording equipment breaks down whilst she is miming into a microphone before an audience. Sometimes, too, we may attempt to persuade others to accept a definition of the situation which is quite different from the one we recognise ourselves: the successful confidence trickster is a highly skilled practitioner of this art. More often, it may be that the interpretation of the situation that we attempt to project is an idealised, rosy-coloured version of what we know from our experience. Such behaviour is characteristic of what are known as the 'higher professions'. Thus, in their public image, judges are impartial founts of wisdom, academics are brilliant and highly knowledgeable. doctors are dedicated single-mindedly to the preservation of life and health, and they are all, of course, exceptionally industrious and unconcerned about their pay.

Whether or not we succeed in presenting desired definitions of the situation, our actions play a significant part in determining the way others we associate with will interpret the situation, and our experience of our own actions and the actions of others we associate with is a major influence in our interpretations and understandings of social life. The roles we have to play in society are not simply set out for us to fit into. They are modified, elaborated, re-created in the course of social intercourse, and it is in the intricate process of social intercourse that human warmth and spontaneity, humour, sentiment, passion, emerge. Such notions as these are, in fact, inconceivable except in terms of human sociality.

Sociological man at last begins to take on human form. But perhaps it may seem that this is true only for the highly personalised world of everyday life, and that the class structure and major institutions of society remain as impersonally deterministic as ever. In the literature of sociology a tendency can in fact be detected to divorce the sociology of everyday life from the analysis of major aspects of the social structure. I have tried to argue that such a divorce is unnecessary, and that, furthermore, our understanding of major aspects of the social structure may be enhanced from the study of the sociology of everyday life. Nor is the individualistic perspective limited to the atomistic world of everyday life. The view of social life in terms of the meaning of events for the individual and the projection of interpretations and definitions for others can be applied to large-scale. groupings and institutions in society. Just as individuals interpret events, there are social interpretations, the 'official' definitions of their activities by large organisations, the interpretations characteristic of particular social

classes, the 'accepted' definitions of the 'authorities'. Individual interpretations of events will always be influenced by current social definitions, but the current social definitions may not be altogether consistent, and the individual may be forced to choose among them. The
sociologist, returning to the perspective of power and conflict, may
note that the ability of individuals, classes, the 'authorities' to persuade
others to accept their world view, their interpretations and definitions
of the situation, may depend largely upon the distribution of power in
society. Hence, certain interpretations of events are seen as authoritative.

For the sociologist, however, there can be no 'authoritative' definitions of the situation to be accepted because of the expertise, superior
qualities, moral or otherwise, or exalted positions of those who pronounce them. He cannot assume that, for example, the social worker's
definition of her client's situation is intrinsically more valid than the
client's own interpretation, or that the teacher's definition of the school
situation is self-evidently more valid than the student's. It is not a
question of pronouncing which view is the closer reflection of reality;
rather, both are to be taken into account in the sociologist's analysis.
The sociologist may nevertheless observe that definitions and interpretations of social reality may be authoritative because of the power
in society of those who pronounce them, rather than because of their
other qualities. The contribution of the individualistic perspective is
the prime place it assigns in the sociologist's analysis to the meanings
and interpretations of events of the people involved in them.

SOCIOLOGICAL 'SCHOOLS'

The sociological man that we observe from our four perspectives on
social life does not represent a complete reflection of human reality.
These perspectives should not be seen as incorporating the viewpoints
of the other social sciences and humanities. In any case, the notion of a
final and complete view is a somewhat utopian and mystical conception: we can never be sure that our analysis and understanding takes
in every point of view, and it is always subject to the limitations of our
experience. But if sociological man is incomplete, he is much more
than an artificial shadow of humanity. In attempting to bring within
his perspective the human warmth, spontaneity and 'private' personality of the individual, the sociologist does not thereby devalue and
destroy such qualities, but, on the contrary, enhances them. The
sociological endeavour is itself an instance of the practical, human,

social activity of members of society in society, their own participation in social life.

The four perspectives presented here provide the sociologist with a framework, a point of departure for the analysis of social life. Further chapters of this book are devoted to elaborating this framework and describing sociological concepts required for its application. This chapter concludes with some general remarks on the scope and limitations of this framework.

The discipline of sociology is often presented as consisting of various 'schools' of sociology – various groupings of sociologists who adhere to several distinctive and often conflicting sociological approaches. The mere names that are applied to such schools – structural functionalism, symbolic interactionism, or more rarely but even more obscurely, positivistic organicism, to quote some of the more wordy – may be sufficient in themselves to inspire awe in the uninitiated. 'Schools' may be identified with the work of their eminent founders, and it is a singularly high mark of academic distinction in more disciplines than sociology to attract 'followers' and come to be regarded as a founder of a school. It is often valuable to examine the work of sociologists in terms of 'schools': such an approach may assist the interpretation of the intellectual antecedents of a given piece of work, and thus be helpful in critical appraisal. Confronted with a new colleague in his university or at a conference the sociologist may seek to know where he stands, and the information that the new colleague is an adherent to a particular school may be highly enlightening. For many sociologists, though, school allegiances may be far from clear, and it then becomes only a fruitless academic game to work out whether they are 'really' followers of this school rather than that, or of this combination of schools rather than that. By overemphasising the division of sociology into schools we may become rigid categorisers, and gain a distorted view of sociology as entirely divided into insulated and warring camps; but worst of all we may lose sight of the overall sociological endeavour.

It would be a mistake to regard the four perspectives presented here as representations of four distinct schools of sociological thought. It is true that the emphasis of each perspective may be more characteristic of certain schools of thought than others, but it is also true that each perspective presented here fails to do more than abstract a selection of the features of any one sociological school, and thus presents a one-sided picture. It is important to make this point, lest the reader be led to believe that, in presenting the approaches of the major sociological schools and arguing that they are complementary, this essay aims at presenting a 'synthesis' of the major conflicting viewpoints in sociology. While sometimes sociologists do set out to provide 'syntheses' of conflicting theoretical viewpoints, such attempts are rather arrogant and probably fruitless. They are arrogant in that the rationale of the 'synthesis' of conflicting viewpoints in sociology is the production of a unified framework which henceforth every sociologist ought to accept as the basis for his work, and they are probably fruitless because in fitting in the elements of the different schools into a theoretically neat framework, the exercise may become increasingly distant from social reality. The supposed synthesis may also turn out to be an attempt to assert the claims of one school over another by showing that the one encompasses and answers all the questions supposedly answered by the others. This may be interesting, but it is not a synthesis. In a more humble sense, however, the practising sociologist is continually synthesising. It is hardly consistent with his intellectual enterprise to choose to throw in his lot with one school rather than another, and henceforth to ignore the rejected schools, to take the side of, say, Karl Marx or Emile Durkheim, as if in some political contest. In solving his sociological research problems, the practising sociologist must use the heritage of sociology as best he can. Perhaps the exponent of one school has contributed something valuable here, and the exponent of another made a remarkable discovery there. In utilising both in his sociological account, the practising sociologist must find some means of accommodating the conflicting intellectual traditions upon which they are based to a consistent framework of analysis. 'Synthesising' the theories of different schools in this limited sense is not, then, some special task reserved for sociological gurus, self-styled or otherwise; it is part of the ongoing activity of practising sociologists, though most of them do not have the presumption to set out their own sociological working framework as I have done here.

Chapter 2 examines the social rules, the norms, that are the basis of order in society. The dominant perspective here is that of society, though the individualistic perspective enters in when individual expectations are contrasted with social norms, and the perspective of power and conflict when norms are considered in relation to social change.

Chapter 3, concerned with influences upon the individual's definition of social reality, relies almost entirely upon the individualistic perspective.

Chapter 4 analyses the concept of social role and related concepts, and it is here that sharp contrasts emerge in the approaches of the society and social system perspectives on the one hand, and the individualistic perspective on the other.

Chapter 5 examines two contrasting approaches to what may be termed the negative features of social organisation: those of alienation, which relates to the perspective of power and conflict, and deviance, which relates to both the perspective of society and the individualistic perspective. It will be seen that each of these terms may serve as a basis for broad characterisations of society, characterisations which are in many ways inherently incompatible and contradictory.

Chapter 6, concerned with power and social inequality, mostly follows the perspective of power and conflict, though the social system perspective serves to provide some contrasts and illustrate some controversies.

Throughout the chapters outlined above, it will become increasingly apparent that the perspectives employed are by no means always compatible. Controversies, incompatibilities and problems of assimilation will reveal further, deeper conflicts and contradictions, ones which have not been alluded to in this introductory chapter. Probably the most serious of these is the problem of the tensions between objectivity and subjectivity in sociology. How, it may be asked, can objectivity be claimed for sociology if at the same time the sociologist argues that social reality must be understood in terms of subjective experience? The final chapter will attempt to deal with this and similar problems, and will conclude with a discussion of the contribution to be made by sociology to social action.

2. The Moral Order of Social Life

The social order is essentially a moral order. Society is ordered according to moral rules. The common-sense, everyday social theory whereby the members of society understand the procedures and operations of social life, the nature of the social world, and the way he and others ought to conduct themselves in the course of social life, is a moral theory. It is not simply that the members of society are constrained in their everyday life by moral codes – their acquired beliefs as to what they ought to do and ought not to do – but that their very construction of the social world is, in a sense, a moral construction. Normally, we think of the world as it is, the factual order, as distinct from ideas about right and wrong, about the way things ought to be and the way people ought to behave. We can distinguish quite simply between what a person is wearing and an evaluation of whether or not he is wearing what he ought to be wearing. In practice, for several reasons, the factual order and the moral order may be indistinct. One reason for this is the tendency for evaluative elements to be included in factual descriptions, as when the décor of a room is described as drab or gaudy, though in principle it may be possible to prevent such evaluations entering factual descriptions. Another reason, and the one which concerns us here, is that the factual order itself is morally endowed: we are morally obliged to accept as facts what everyone else accepts as facts. People who challenge the accepted factual order (though this may be permissible to a limited extent in certain areas defined as scientific) may offend moral sentiments in the same way as those who challenge the explicitly moral codes. Copernicus was persecuted because he challenged the accepted view of the time that the sun went round the earth and other scientific discoverers have met similar, if milder, fates. The hippie rejects conventional morality, but the reaction against him is perhaps not merely directed against his flouting of conventional morals, but also against his challenge to accepted definitions of the nature of society and the social order.

Similarly, the political radical offends in part also because he challenges accepted definitions of the nature of society and the social order: for him the work and leisure, comfort and conformity, affluence and emulation of the middle-class suburbanite may seem an alienated, dehumanised form of existence, dependent upon the material depriva-tion of others.

Thus, as those who challenge the factual order offend moral senti-ments, so it may be shown that the factual order is morally endowed. Further illustration may be provided with more concrete examples. A young person who has been brought up to believe that the society in which he lives is one of democracy and equal opportunity for all may find simple descriptions of the extent of inequalities in his society as offensive. For him, the description of social inequality is not a proper way to view the social order. The sociology student may have hitherto regarded the ducks on the wall and floral wallpaper at his home as not very aesthetic, but with some understanding of status symbolism their reality is dramatically transformed: they no longer represent what seemed to him to be the rather old-fashioned choices of his parents: instead they now appear as impersonal manifestations of the determin-ism of social class. Such a transformation of reality may well seem to be offensive.

In everyday life, an acquaintance who continually challenges our conception of social reality, who always sees ulterior motives, who is constantly aware of conspiracies around him, whose conceptions of himself and ourselves are so patently incompatible with our own, may well cause us considerable anxiety. Such people may eventually be defined as paranoic and confined to mental hospitals, but in our inter-action with them we may sometimes be led to doubt our own judge-ment, our conception of social reality, possibly our own sanity. The behaviour of such people represents an offence against the moral order, not because they engage in immoral actions – though they may do – but because they disturb our morally endowed conception of social reality.

The moral order of social life, then, does not refer merely to sets of moral and ethical codes to which we adhere in certain aspects of our conduct: indeed, such consciously articulated codes may be idealised prescriptions which bear little relationship in practice to social conduct – as is the case for several contemporary versions of Christianity. The moral order of social life is far more penetrating. In addition to implicit or explicit rules prescribing social conduct which include much more than would be conventionally regarded as moral rules, the socially shared definitions of the nature of social reality are themselves morally endowed.

The sociologist may approach the moral order of social life by considering the socially prescribed rules for social conduct and procedural rules for ordering social reality. Such rules are known as norms. Sociologists usually distinguish norms from moral values. Put simply, while norms represent moral rules to which the individual may or may not conform, values represent the ends of social action to which individuals may be committed. One conforms or deviates from the norms which prohibit stealing, but one is or is not committed to values such as private property, freedom, or democracy. Norms are, in a sense, secondary to values in that they may represent means of achieving values, as for the Christian who lives righteously in order to achieve grace, or the business executive who works hard to achieve 'success'. Similarly, norms may be seen as derivatives of values, as in the case of laws against theft which may be seen as derivatives of the value of the rights of ownership of property. However, the concept of value in sociology and the relation between norms and values raises complex issues, and here it will simplify matters considerably and serve our purpose adequately to focus the discussion solely upon social norms.

SOCIAL RULES: NORMS

It is the perspective of 'society' that focuses our attention upon social norms, for it is in the form of social norms that 'society' confronts the individual as external and constraining.

Norms, the rules of procedure and conduct in social life, are inherently social. Social in that not only do they refer to social life, but that they are themselves the products of social life. They are a part of 'society', generated in the course of social life, prescribing the scope and limits of conduct in social life. The individual is born into a society and is socialised to accept the rules of that society, which are there before him. He internalises the rules, accepts them as standards of right and wrong, and is controlled by them not only by the fear of causing offence to others, but also by his own feelings of guilt incurred by the infraction of norms. For example, in a Western society in which the norm of the virtues of hard work is dominant, the individual may feel guilty if he is not 'doing anything', and such guilt may even extend to his leisure time. Thus, if we follow Emile Durkheim, we may see social norms as external to individuals, restraining them and controlling their behaviour. That individuals may not experience such pressures or coercion is because they have internalised the norms, have accepted them as their own standards. Such general propositions as these do not take into account the wide diversity of the norms of different groups in any society, but serve to establish the general principle as to the social nature of social norms. Throughout life, the individual is socialised to accept the norms of the diverse social groups in which he may participate – the family, the school peer group, the factory shop-floor, the working men's club, and so forth. Social norms may sometimes appear to be formulated deliberately by an individual or group of individuals, as when the legislative chamber enacts laws, the military dictator pronounces edicts, or when the founder members of a social club work out a constitution and a set of rules. However, if such rules are not reinforced by social pressures they cannot be regarded as social norms. The military dictator may enforce conformity to a rule that no one should be allowed out of their homes after dark by seeing that those who don't conform are shot: the rule may thus be observed but is not a social norm: it has no basis in the order of social life, and its observance is simply a product of physical force, though this is not to say that over time rules based on physical force may not acquire the character of social norms. Often where rules are pronounced or laws enacted which are inconsistent with social norms, they will not be reinforced by social pressures, and in the absence of physical coercion, may fail to be observed. In Britain, the effectiveness of laws against driving under the influence of alcohol has been limited by social norms to some groups in society, for whom driving to a country pub or to the house of a friend for alcoholic drinks is an approved social pastime. For the individual member of such groups, not to engage in behaviour which has the result of him driving under the influence of alcohol may result in social disapproval. Generally speaking, however, it may be said that enacted laws are likely to relate to at least some aspects of prevailing sets of social norms. The individuals who get together to frame the rules of a new social club will be constrained and influenced in their actions by the prevailing climate of norms in their social situation, and in fact this would apply even in the case of a 'deviant' or illegal organisation – perhaps a movement committed to the overthrow of the prevailing social order. In the case of the social club, the framed rules may in part reflect prevailing social norms, and in part consist of idealised maxims – references to God, country, fraternity, and such like – which are of no direct relevance to the social order of the club. However, once the social club is organised and develops, then it may generate its own social norms which may or may not be related to the formal rules. Members come to recognise what sort of behaviour is appropriate in the club, and what sort of behaviour is out of place. Certain forms of humour will be well received, others will be seen as in 'bad taste'. In certain respects, what is appropriate behaviour in the context of the club may depart somewhat from what is regarded as appropriate outside, in everyday life. Thus in terms of 'conventional' standards, certain eccentricities of dress may be expected of the member of the sailing club. Similarly, in the amateur dramatic society, forms of flirtation and physical contact may be permissible which would not be outside the society's activities.

IDEALS AND REALITIES:
Subsistent norms and normative maxims
Once the social nature of norms is appreciated, then some of the difficulties facing the sociologist in defining and observing the actual norms of any social group or society become apparent. First of all, social norms cannot be equated with formal written laws and social rules. This is not only because social norms include far more than formalised written codes, but because the formalised written codes may sometimes be out of step with or even quite irrelevant to the norms of social life. But beyond the formally recorded codes of social conduct we may be mistaken in even equating verbal statements of social norms with the norms themselves. Theodore Geiger[1] has distinguished between actual norms, which he refers to as *subsistent norms*, and the verbal expression of norms, referred to as *normative maxims*, and shown that the relationship between the two is far from one of simple correspondence. A normative maxim that stealing is wrong may, for example, be accompanied by subsistent norms whereby certain forms of stealing, such as the taking of things from one's workplace that would 'only be thrown away', or failing to point out when one is undercharged, are not socially disapproved. Normative maxims may sometimes be found independent of any actual subsistent norm. This occurs when beliefs are current about the way people ought to behave which either are impossible to conform to in practice, or are so vague and ambiguous as to have no practical effect on the conduct of social life. The maxim 'love thy neighbour as thyself' could be seen as such a maxim. From at least one interpretation, its demands would

seem to be impossible, and so many interpretations are possible – even the Spanish inquisitor might have believed that he conformed to it – that it cannot be seen to relate to any specific actual subsistent norm: the verbalisation is not reflected in the actual ordering of social life. Conversely, if the maxim were such that it would be impossible not to conform with it, then it would not refer to a subsistent norm either. Conformity to it would be a product not of the constraints of social life, of society, but of physiological or other limitations. It is not easy to think of examples: it is perhaps not surprising that few people take pains to tell people not to do what they could not possibly do anyway. Yet the high incidence of certain forms of crime among certain social groups and its relative low incidence among others may relate not so much to the different moralities and social norms of these groups but to the fact that for some people certain forms of crime may be impossible because of the lack of necessary resources. Professional thieving presupposes some means of disposing of the proceeds, counterfeiting requires considerable skill, and fraudulent conversion is only possible for those entrusted with the funds and resources of others. These are, perhaps, rather limited examples but they do serve to make the point that conformity to a normative maxim may be dictated by physical rather than social factors.

The expression of normative maxims, verbalised statements of norms, cannot, then, be assumed to indicate the presence of actual subsistent norms. It is also the case that subsistent norms may be present without corresponding normative maxims. By no means all the norms that are operative and adhered to in social life are verbalised. If we asked anyone – even a sociologist – to write down all the social norms that he saw applying to him in the various spheres of his social life, he would be quite unable to comply with our demand. For any individual, the norms are so intricate and so many as to make the task impossible. Even a complete list of verbally recognised norms, the verbal maxims, would leave out a whole range of norms which are not explicitly verbalised, rules of conduct which are unnoticed, taken-for-granted, so obvious that they do not appear as rules at all. It may seem strange that people should obey rules that they do not explicitly recognise and cannot formulate in verbal terms, but the ordering of social life is highly complex and intricate, and cannot be reduced by the sociologist or anyone else to simple sets of rules which can be recorded verbally.

If people cannot verbalise and consciously recognise certain social norms, then we may well wonder how it is that people abide by them. If they are not recognised as rules, then who is to know whether they are being observed or not? It may seem that we are retreating from the realities of social life into mysticism. The answer is that social norms must in fact be recognised by the participants in social life: they can operate only in so far as there are social pressures upon the individual, pressures from his associates and members of social groups who do recognise the norms. However, they are recognised in their breach and not in their observance. The member of the social club may be unable to provide a verbal or written record of all the norms operating in the club: but he can recognise when someone is out of step, when someone has gone too far, or when something is out of place. Some social norms may be taken for granted and thus are unnoticed while they are followed, but once they are breached they can no longer be taken for granted. The patient in the surgery might find some aspect of the doctor's behaviour – perhaps the doctor has produced some pornographic magazines and suggested that these are a good form of treatment – quite incompatible with his expectations, and quite out of place. Henceforth he may now start to question a number of hitherto taken-for-granted features of the situation. Was that examination and questioning really necessary for medical practice? Why does he keep operating that switch? Is he really a proper doctor in the first place? And is this really a surgery anyway? Perhaps it is in fact some experimental (scientific or otherwise) studio or laboratory into which the hapless patient has been lured. The breaching of taken-for-granted social norms may throw into a focus a whole set of taken-for-granted assumptions. The fragile ordering of social life may well depend upon such assumptions. It is important, therefore, that the sociological analysis of social norms should not be restricted to those that are explicitly verbalised.

SANCTIONS

The participant in social life recognises social norms when they are breached. But how, we may ask, is the sociologist to recognise them? In his study of a social organisation, his experience of the organisation may be insufficient for him to be sensitive to the out of place, the discordant, and the unseemly in social conduct. Yet the sociologist can rely on other participants in the organisation to recognise the breach of social norms and he may observe their reactions, which will consist of the imposition of penalties and sanctions. Breaches of social norms are always met with sanctions, which may range from mild expressions of social disapproval through ostracism to imprisonment and execution. The very concept of social norm implies that norms are reinforced by social pressures upon the individual. By focusing on the sanctions accompanying social norms we can clearly define the scope of their influence in social life.

Uniformities in the behaviour of individuals in the conduct of social life may be regarded as a product of the adherence to social norms. The view might therefore be taken that the presence of such uniformities – uniformities of dress, of forms of address, of the behaviour of men towards women, and parents towards their children – indicates the presence of social norms. In most cases this will probably be the case but not always. The test for whether uniformities of conduct represent the adherence to social norms is whether behaviour which deviates from such uniformities is subjected to social sanctions. At the meeting of a social group, for example, we might be mistaken in assuming that because everyone sits cross-legged on the floor there is a social norm requiring this. We could only make this assumption if we were to observe social sanctions against a member who did not conform to this uniformity. If he were told to behave himself, asked whether he felt ill or tired, or were treated in some other special negative way, then the presence of a norm would be indicated. But if his different posture or stature gave rise to no reaction on the part of his fellows, then the uniformity would not be based upon a social norm. Similarly, the sociologist might observe uniformities in domestic appearances and life styles on a new housing estate: all the gardens may have similar layouts, and be tended according to a regular pattern: lawns mown on Saturday afternoons. The motor-cars, too, may be of much the same age, size and design, and washed on Sunday mornings. Only if we can observe the applications of sanctions against the non-conformist: if, for example, the resident whose garden has no neat lawn but a mass of dahlias, or possibly cabbages, whose car is much older than other people's, is socially disapproved, regarded as different by the other residents, perhaps lowering the 'tone' of the neighbourhood, then it would be appropriate to regard the observed uniformities as indicating the presence of social norms.

The focus on the sanctions accompanying norms throws further light on the distinction made between subsistent norms and actual norms. If behaviour which is not in conformity with the prescriptions of a normative maxim does not incur any social penalty, then it would be evident that the normative maxim does not relate to any actual subsistent norm. Thus, the Christian maxim of 'turning the other cheek' may be verbally approved in some social groups whereas at the same time behaviour which is clearly incompatible with this maxim may not only not evoke any sanctions, but even evoke praise as socially approved conduct, indicating that the individual is able to 'stand up for himself'. In such cases, it is clear that the normative maxim does not express any actual subsistent norm.

Sometimes the individual may be faced with conflicting normative demands. For example, suppose that at a chess tournament a man takes a telephone call from the wife of one of the contestants, a close friend of his, asking for her husband to come to the telephone immediately as there has been a serious accident at home involving the children. Should the man immediately do as the woman has asked, and thus interrupt a game in the tournament, where even the rustle of a sweet paper may cause offence, or should he neglect the urgent request of his friend's wife? In this case subsistent norms are clearly in conflict.

In some cases such conflicts are resolved by reference to other norms which state that certain norms take precedence over others. The child in the classroom who shouts out when the class has been told to be silent will be more than forgiven if the shouting is to inform the teacher that a cupboard is on fire. Conflicting norms often confront individuals as conflicting expectations of them in the roles they are playing, and where this is the case can be understood as role conflict, which is discussed in Chapter 4.

In developing classifications of social norms, sociologists have usually focused upon the nature and strength of the sanctions accompanying the norms. One well-known classification, formulated by the early American sociologist William Graham Sumner, distinguishes norms as *folkways* and *mores*. Folkways are standard practices, customs and conventions to which general conformity is expected. The individual whose non-conformity to folkways is noticeable may merely be regarded as eccentric and subjected to mild forms of social disapproval. Conformity to *mores*, however, is a much more serious moral requirement, and failure to observe them evokes strong moral sentiments, and consequently, severe sanctions. This classification is rather crude, and is one of degree, dependent upon the relative strength of sanctions, rather than one of distinct kinds of norms. Another classification of social norms according to the strength of sanctions has been proposed

by Ralf Dahrendorf. He has distinguished three kinds of expectations*
attached to the performance of social roles: 'must' expectations, 'shall'
expectations, and 'can' expectations.[2] The clear and simple labels he
has used indicate the relative strengths of the sanctions for each type
of norm. 'Must' expectations are reinforced by legal or quasi-legal
sanctions, and refer to the social rules that we must comply with if we
are not to be prosecuted in the law courts, or brought before a tribunal,
as in the case of some professionals, for improper or 'infamous'
conduct. 'Shall' expectations refer to the minimum requirements of the
social roles we perform. In the case of our occupational roles, they are
the requirements that must be met if we are to avoid being sacked or
having our pay reduced. The sanctions attached to 'shall' expectations
are purely social, rather than legal or quasi-legal. Those who fail to
conform to these, their minimum role requirements, may lose their
jobs, be ostracised, or be labelled by their fellows as idle, irresponsible,
or incompetent. 'Can' expectations refer to those ways of performing
social roles over and above minimum requirements which gain social
approval for the individual. As Dahrendorf says:

> The man who never does more than what is absolutely necessary
> must have very effective alternative sources of gratification to
> remain unaffected by the disapproval of his fellowmen.[3]

In a social group where generosity is socially approved, it may not be
necessary for the individual to show evidence of his generosity continually in order to avoid social disapproval, but where his actions are
regarded as generous, they will gain for him social approval. Sanctions
attached to 'can' expectations tend to be positive rather than negative:
it is not so much that those who do not meet them are socially pena-
lised, but rather that those who do meet them are socially rewarded.
We must, however, be wary of placing too narrow an interpretation
upon expectations of performing more than the minimum requirements
of social roles, especially in the context of occupational roles. For work
behaviour which from one point of view may seem to be exemplary,
industrious and conscientious work, may, from the point of view of
the members of the social group in which this conduct takes place, be
regarded as 'rate busting', selling out to the bosses and letting down
one's fellow workers. Such conduct, evoking sanctions such as ostra-

---

* These are treated here as equivalent to social norms. Dahrendorf does not
distinguish between norms and expectations as is done here (see pp. 49–52).

cism or 'being sent to Coventry', would be contrary to the norms of the social group in which it takes place.

Norms are sometimes classified not so much according to the strength of the sanctions, but according to the method whereby the sanctions are imposed, or the agencies which have the responsibility of imposing sanctions. A basic distinction can be made between sanctions that are legally or quasi-legally imposed and those which are socially imposed. Dahrendorf's distinction between must and shall expectations in part reflects such a distinction. In the former, specialised agencies – police, law courts, tribunals – are developed to impose sanctions; in the latter there are no specialised enforcement agencies. Socially imposed sanctions operate through social pressures upon the individual in the course of everyday social interaction and are not the responsibility of specially designated individuals. There may, however, be some individuals who come to be regarded as moral leaders. Included among these would be the one who speaks first about 'goings on' that others have become aware of but have chosen to ignore, not wishing to initiate reproving action themselves. A number of residents in a street may be willing to sign a petition protesting about the activities of a despised family in the street, but few may be prepared to draw up the petition in the first place.

The social process whereby sanctions are imposed is itself governed by social norms. The procedural rules which regulate the agencies responsible for imposing legal or quasi-legal sanctions are sometimes referred to as secondary norms. Law-enforcement agencies may be governed by a whole set of such rules, prescribing such things as permissible ways of obtaining evidence and confessions. Some such secondary norms may themselves be backed up by legal sanctions, as in the case of the British policeman who uses physical violence to extract a confession, or by quasi-legal sanctions, as in the case of the policeman who is punished by his superior for offences against police discipline. Others may only be socially sanctioned, as is the over-zealous police recruit who is ridiculed by his colleagues for making all possible arrests. The point has been made that formal written rules cannot be equated with social norms, and this is as true for secondary as for other norms. The following quotation from a study of police activity provides an illustration:

Policemen feel that they are forced to live on the fringes of the law: 'You can't play it to the book. You'd never get anywhere in a job like this.' . . . Policemen were cynical about the hypocrisy of a society which paid lip service to one set of rules but put pressure on them to work by another. . . .[4]

PROCEDURAL RULES AND THE ORDER OF EVERYDAY LIFE

One important set of norms which is unlikely to be accompanied by verbal maxims, but to be very much taken for granted and unnoticed, is that of the procedural rules for the ordering of social reality in everyday life. The very procedures whereby we construct our definitions of social reality may be seen to be governed by social norms. We interpret events in terms of their correspondence with what is expected to happen in the future, we interpret them in a chronological time sequence. We relate events to each other and to their environment in terms of common-sense notions of cause and effect. We frequently assume that things will continue to happen very much as they have happened in the past. These are some of the procedural rules that are followed in the ordering of the social world, the construction of social reality in everyday life, and, indeed, such rules are very necessary for the perception of an ordered social world. Those who fail to abide by such procedural rules will be subjected to varying social sanctions: the person who is not able to see common-sense causality, to 'put two and two together', is seen as lacking common sense: the person who fails to accept the assumption that things will proceed as they have in the past, the husband who asks his wife whether she will cook his dinner when she has done so every day for twenty years, the grocer who asks his regular cash customer whether she intends to pay for her purchases, will at the very least annoy his associates. The person who disregards so many of the procedural rules that his ordering of social reality is no longer comparable to those of his associates will pursue a very hazardous social career, one which in all likelihood will end in a mental hospital.

The examples given here may seem so patently obvious as to be quite trivial. Of course people will be irritated by the behaviour of those who do not grasp or accept what is obvious to everyone else. But the attention of the sociologist may not be quite so trivial. The point is that procedures whereby social reality, the factual order, is defined, are normative, themselves a product of social life. The members of a society other than our own will not only have different ideas about the way people ought to behave, about what is good and what is bad, but may also define social reality differently because they have different ideas about how this ought to be done. Even within a society, different social groups may not only have different ideas about what ought to be done, but also have different conceptions of the facts of the situation. Norms in social life define not only the way we ought to behave, but also the way we ought to see the factual order of things.

There may be occasions when we are confronted with situations in which the procedural norms for interpreting social reality do not seem to apply, or to work. In such situations we are unable to impose any order upon the situation, and are faced with meaningless and purpose-less sensations. Suppose, for example, at the theatre, we find that as the play is about to begin we become aware of a group of people standing and shouting in an aisle, who seem to be insulting and shouting obscenities to all and sundry around them. The curtain then opens revealing one or two actors on the stage, but these are immediately descended upon by the same group from the audience who pull them off the stage into the auditorium. In the ensuing mêlée, as members of the audience, we will be at a loss to comprehend what is going on, unless we have gained some cues that what we are witnessing *is* part of the theatrical performance that we have come to see. It may, of course, be the technique of the experimental theatre company to avoid giving such cues, to disturb the member of the audience rather than to allow him to sit back, impose his conventional theatrical definition of the situation and thereby apply the appropriate procedural norms.

The report of an experiment provides a more detailed illustration.[5] Students were invited to participate in an experiment, the purpose of which, they were told, was to develop a new quick technique of psycho-therapy. They were asked to think over some personal problem, and to ask the therapist ten questions, all of which could be, and would be, answered with a straight 'yes' or 'no'. The 'therapy' was conducted through a loudspeaker and microphones, so that the student was not in the same room as the therapist, and never saw him: the only response to his questions was the 'yes' or 'no' from the loudspeaker. Now, in fact, the answers given by the therapist had nothing to do with the questions asked, but were given in a prearranged sequence. For some students, the yeses and noes were randomly distributed; others received a 'yes' to every question, and yet others, a 'no' to every question. Objectively, the answers given were meaningless. The students were asked to record what they understood the therapist to be telling them, and at the end of the session to summarise what they had learnt from it. Some students were able to order and interpret the answers, and thus render them compatible with the interpretation of the situation as a therapeutic interview, but there were frequent difficulties. Some students found the answers they were given to be contradictory, though even here an interpretation consistent with the therapeutic interview situation might be attempted: perhaps this had some deep purpose for the therapy, or perhaps this was just what psychologists were like. But in some cases the meaninglessness of the answers altogether disrupted the students' ordering of the situation: how could it be therapy when the answers were so pointless? Was there really a therapist at all?

Situations such as these, where we are confronted with things that seem meaningless, purposeless and chaotic, occur where our procedural rules for interpreting events do not seem to apply. Sociologists may use the concept of *anomie*, which, in basic terms, means a state of normlessness. In a situation of *anomie*, the fragile social order is disrupted. *Anomie* may describe situations not only where procedural norms for the ordering of social reality do not seem to work, but also where for one reason or another norms regulating behaviour, moral conduct, are weakened: it is, in fact, more frequently employed for this latter purpose. Emile Durkheim, who originally formulated the concept in sociological terms, showed, in a famous study of his,[6] how rises in suicide rates could be explained in terms of the weakening of the ties of social norms upon the individual. Following the tradition of Durkheim, *anomie* has been a major concept for sociological explanations of crime and deviance, and is discussed in this context (Ch. 5, pp. 126–8). We have introduced the concept here to indicate that if the individual is indeed constantly subject to social norms – much more than in conventionally defined areas of moral conduct – then the normative order itself is always subject to disruption. Furthermore, just as norms are social, products of society rather than the individual, *anomie* refers to a social situation – a situation in which norms are weak – rather than to the feelings of individuals.

EXPECTATIONS

Norms are social, products of social interaction, of society rather than the individual. The emphasis of the preceding section may seem to favour the conception of sociological man as a socially determined, rather mechanical product. For the individual, the normative order is there prior to his participation in social life. At the same time, it should be recognised that norms are created only through the conscious activities of people, and that the normative order changes as a consequence of these activities. Norms confront the individual as external, social, not of his own design, but to suggest that norms could be other than the creations of individual people in the course of social life would be to retreat into mysticism – to suggest that 'society' has some life and existence of its own independent of the individuals of which it is composed. The focus on expectations is useful for providing some indication of the processes whereby norms are created and changed through social action. It introduces the individualistic perspective, the focus on the individual's perception and interpretation of the situation, and hence his influence, into the discussion.

It is first necessary to make the rather elementary distinction between factual, predictive expectations and prescriptive, or moral expectations. The first of these is concerned with what people are actually likely to do, and the second with what people ought to do. Taking factual expectations first, it may be said that our participation in social life depends upon our ability to predict how others will respond to our actions, irrespective of our ideas as to the way they really ought to respond. The radical politician may perceive that whereas people ought to respond favourably to a revolutionary socialist appeal, in fact they will not, and that, therefore, if he is to achieve any influence, his appeal must be modified in the light of his expectations as to the way it will actually be received. The teacher may come to expect that his 'C' stream class will not show the enthusiasm for academic work that they ought to, and will modify his methods accordingly.

Prescriptive, or moral, expectations may be regarded as the subjective counterparts to social norms. If we accept particular social norms, then we may have the expectation that the behaviour of others with whom we associate will be in accordance with these norms, and we may perceive that these others expect us to conform to these social norms as well. If norms are social, then expectations are held only by individuals. At the same time, it would be a mistake to regard expectations as mechanical reflections of norms. In everyday life, our expectations of others and the expectations we perceive that others have of us cover a far wider range of activities than do social norms. In intimate social relationships, expectations develop through detailed knowledge of the personal qualities and life histories of those with whom we interact. We may expect an intimate friend to smile at the mention of the name of a place which has mutual humorous associations, to avoid particular topics of conversation which might seem innocuous to a stranger, and to sit in a particular chair without being told. Such personal expectations are much more fluid than social norms, and are subject to continual modification in the course of our experiences.

While the distinction between factual and moral expectations may seem to be quite clear and sharp, in practice this can become somewhat blurred. Thus we may expect people to laugh at our jokes because we predict that they will find them funny. But even if we allow that our jokes may fall flat, we might still expect (in this case a normative expectation) our associates to laugh because it would be impolite for them not to do so. Factual expectations may well influence and modify moral expectations. Generally speaking, it is disconcerting for us when other people's behaviour falls outside the range of our predictions, and there is thus a tendency for us to disapprove of social behaviour which is quite inconsistent with our factual expectations: people ought to behave more or less as we expect them to. Thus, a woman may believe that her husband ought to be home at six o'clock for dinner not because she would disapprove of a later time, but because that is the time he always comes home. The psychiatrist may expect his patients to display sets of symptoms which are consistent with his categories of clinical analysis, and may be disconcerted by – and perhaps less sympathetic towards – those who don't. The theme of this chapter is that the social order is a moral order, that our social construction of the world as it is is also, in a sense, a construction of the world as it ought to be. Factual expectations in everyday life, based upon our constructions of social reality, always contain some moral component.

The emphasis here on the moral aspect of expectations should not lead us to the view that expectations are always consistent with given social norms. One source of inconsistency may be the variations in individual perceptions and interpretation of social norms. In the university, for example, adherence to norms of academic scholarship may mean for one academic that all his work is backed up by vast bibliographies and detailed referencing, but for another that his work shows originality. The one interprets the norms to mean that he must not say anything without being able to cite someone who has said it before, whereas the other interprets them as meaning that the value of his work is to be judged in terms of what he says that someone has not said before. Now it might be argued that the example here really illustrates conflicting norms in academic life, rather than interpretations of norms. This may be so, but the difference may still derive from differing interpretations of given social norms, or more basically from the expeciations of significant individuals – those who decide upon academic awards and preferment – and the way these expectations are perceived by others.

Expectations may furthermore be consciously in contradiction to social norms. The schoolteacher, especially if he is a headmaster or in an influential position, may choose to flout traditional school norms, and his pupils may recognise that what is expected of them has changed: perhaps they are no longer expected to be submissive to authority, regimented and orderly and always to do and say exactly what they are told, and consequently their expectations of the teacher may change as well. In the home, parents' expectations for their children may consciously depart from the social norms for children's behaviour. The middle-class parent may choose not to expect his child to be motivated in his education to 'getting ahead'. (Working-class parents tend not to have such expectations anyway.) Children and adolescents may develop expectations of authority figures in society which are consciously at odds with social norms. Individual expectations are always to some degree constrained by the normative order, for it is the normative order that sets the framework for them, but they are continually modified in the course of social action. Expectations of children in the school situation will be modified and changed by the action of teachers, and by the action of themselves towards each other. When people have expectations which are inconsistent with social norms, then there will be a tendency for the norms themselves to change.

The consideration of expectations as individualised counterparts to social norms goes some way to balance an otherwise somewhat rigid, determinist 'societal' view of social life structured by social norms which are external to and semi-independent of individuals. Norms are external to and independent of the individual in so far as they confront the individual as such: what 'society', as opposed to particular people, expects of one. The contrast between social norms and individual expectations also provides a pointer to the conflict, the dialectical relationship, between the individual and society. I shall return to this theme in the discussion of role playing (Chapter 4, pp. 80–85). As will be seen there, roles can be defined as sets of expectations.

NORMS AND SOCIAL CHANGE

A brief examination of the relationship between norms and social change enables us to introduce the perspective of power and conflict into the discussion of social norms.

If norms are the basis for the ordering of social life, then it would seem to follow that social change, change in the structure of society, occurs as a result of changes in social norms. Such a view would fit in rather well with the opinions of certain contemporary self-appointed moral leaders, opinions which gather a fair measure of popular support. The gist of these opinions, put very crudely, is that contemporary trends which represent changes for the worse, such as the increasing incidence of industrial strikes, crime, and sexual permissiveness, are the result of moral decay, and can be reversed only by some sort of moral regeneration. Nor is the opinion that contemporary social ills are to be remedied by moral reform held only by reactionaries. For some Americans, the conduct of the Vietnam war was a reflection of the extreme immorality of the political élite and military leadership. There are British radicals, too, who see the decline of membership and activism in the Labour Party as partly caused by the weak moral fibre of the party leadership.

American sociology has tended to be dominated by the view that social change follows more or less from normative changes. In this view it is deviance, in the form of the rejection of existing social norms and the creation of new ones, that is the major force for social change.[7] But the argument that social norms are the basis for the ordering of social life suggests no more than that social change is accompanied by changes in the normative order. Only if the view is taken that the structure of society is ultimately derived from social norms, does it follow that social change is produced by normative change. In the preceding section the point was made that individual expectations may be contrary to social norms and may be influential in bringing about changes in social norms. It is not difficult to see that some individuals, by virtue of their positions in society, can be more influential in such changes than others. The progressive headmaster may be able to sweep away many of the traditional norms of the school, but against his opposition a group of sixth-formers are likely to meet with little success in the same endeavour. Very simply, this follows from the distribution of power in the school. Normative changes are more likely to be brought about by those in positions of power in society than by the powerless, and major changes in the normative order are more likely to follow from changes in the power structure than to bring about such changes. If powerful groups in society are in strong positions to influence and bring about changes in social norms, then they are also able to be influential in preserving social norms of which they approve. The genesis and development of social norms in society cannot, therefore, be understood without reference to the distribution of power in society, and it is not very fruitful to consider the relation between changes in the normative order and changes in the structure of society without reference to power.*

If it is true that social norms are dependent upon the distribution of power in society, it might appear that those who seek to bring about changes in society by moral pressures are mistaken. This would be too simplistic a view, for moral appeals may generate social action which brings about major social changes. The reliance upon moral appeals is only mistaken if it is believed that the moral order can be changed without changing the structure of society and the distribution of power. It is mistaken, for example, when reformers believe that the conduct of a political or military régime may be changed by an appeal to the moral sentiments of the members of the régime. It is, for example, a current myth in some circles that governments can be made to respond to 'world public opinion' (which usually means the opinions of the liberal middle class of the West). A cursory glance at recent events in Czechoslovakia, Greece, Vietnam and Bangladesh suffices to demonstrate the unreality of this myth. It is not that political élites are cynical exponents of naked power and respond to nothing other than a challenge to their power, though it is sometimes difficult not to come to this conclusion. Rather, it is that they ignore such moral appeals because their construction of social reality, of the factual and moral order, is different from that of their critics, and they are therefore unaffected by their critics. Their conception of social reality and their morality is more likely to change through their experiences when their exercise of power is threatened or removed.

---

* The relationship of power to norms and the social order is discussed further in Chapter 6 (pp. 136–41).

3. Social Definitions and Perspectives

Our interpretation of social reality depends upon our frame of reference, our perspective, or the standpoint which we take. Without some perspective, we cannot order the various stimuli impinging upon our sense. This book began by setting out the perspectives of the sociologist. A distinctive feature of the sociologist's perspectives is that they are able to take into account and encompass everyday perspectives on social reality. The sociologist sees the social order and the course of social life as very much dependent upon people's definitions and interpretations of the social order. This chapter seeks to examine some of the processes whereby the individual member of society defines social reality and interprets his social situation, and thus focuses almost entirely upon the individualistic perspective. Two sociological concepts provide the key to this process, the 'definition of the situation' and 'reference groups'.

DEFINING THE SITUATION

The pioneer American sociologist W. I. Thomas showed that the individual's definition of the situation provides the basis for the way he acts in a given situation. A great variety of activity may be explained if we are able to understand the way those whose actions we wish to explain define the situation. For example, the lecturer may be exasperated when he realises that the student's essay he is marking is copied verbatim from a book: laziness, deceit, or contempt for 'academic' values may suggest themselves as causes for this, otherwise it may seem inexplicable. However, an understanding of the student's definition of the situation may lead to a rather different conclusion. For the student may see the purpose of academic study defined as the learning of what the 'authorities' in his discipline have pronounced, and the purpose of essay-writing, therefore, as the reproduction of the expositions of these 'authorities'. Now he may have heard of the idea of transposing the works of the 'authorities' into his own words, but, given the way the situation is defined, this may seem to be no more than a stylistic ritual. How could he be expected to improve upon the work of the 'authorities'? So, if a given piece of literature is appropriate in length and content for the essay topic, why not reproduce it? Far from showing contempt for 'academic' values, the student may believe that his actions are entirely consistent with them as he understands them. His actions are consistent with his definition of the situation, and he may believe that this definition is shared by his teachers, because he will have derived it at least partly from his understanding of them.

The focus of sociology on the definition of the situation directs attention to the individual. It is the individual member of society who formulates his own interpretation of events and the actions of others, and it is he who defines the situation. He does not, of course, do this in a social vacuum, for he will be influenced by social norms in defining the elements of the situation and in evaluating them. Yet in the last analysis the emerging definition is dependent upon the interpretation and understanding of the individual. Even the influence of social norms depends upon the individual's own interpretation of them

Social life may be seen to be dependent upon the sharing of definitions of the situation, and, indeed, it is not difficult to realise that, without shared definitions, social intercourse is impossible. In order to communicate with other people, we must assume that their view of the situation resembles ours at least in certain essential respects. A conversation between gardeners on methods of dealing with weeds would be rather fruitless if they did not share a definition of what sorts of plants were to be regarded as weeds. To smooth the course of social life, and to avoid making life difficult, we may even go out of our way to ignore or turn a blind eye to things which may seem inconsistent with the definition of the situation we assume that we are supposed to accept and that everyone else accepts. Thus, the middle-aged lady may pretend not to notice the pile of racing newspapers, the concealment of which has been neglected in preparing for the vicar's tea party. The slumbers of a colleague at a professional meeting may be ignored by his fellows, who will strive to ensure that no remarks are addressed to him which would make his state a focus of attention and thus perhaps disrupt the serious proceedings. One reason why people often ignore things that are inconsistent with the given definition of the situation is that incongruous revelations may be most embarrassing for all. It is less painful to eat the gooseberry pie sugared with salt than to witness the public revelation of the hostess's error.

The tendency of people to go along with definitions of the situation that they assume that they are supposed to accept is frequently exploited in the realms of theatrical comedy. Situational comedy relies very much for its humour on the reactions of people to glaring inconsistencies. When a pair of feet descends into the fireplace, or an apparently ownerless hand appears from behind a curtain and removes fruit from a dish, it is not so much the incidents themselves, but the reactions of the other actors to them that make the audience laugh.

Quite often in everyday social life we not only take for granted that things are what they seem, what we think they are supposed to be, but deliberately try to ignore or explain away evidence confronting us that might lead us to think that things are other than what they seem. This may well be one reason why confidence tricksters are able to succeed in persuading their victims to accept false definitions of the situation. In reading of such events in the newspapers, we may wonder at the apparent gullibility of the victim: why were no credentials asked for? How could *anyone* believe such an unlikely story? But when we are reading the report, it is defined for us as the report of the operation of a confidence trick. In the actual situation, we may be much more likely to give the benefit of the doubt, and to assume that things are what they seem. The example of the confidence trick also serves to show how definitions of the situation may be manipulated: situations may be contrived so that things are quite different from what they seem to be. Erving Goffman has described the process whereby appearances are manipulated so that they appear as normal when they are anything but normal.[1]

An extreme example is where the individual in the street observes an apparently unrelated and unconnected collection of individuals going about normal everyday activities: in fact, they may have all been collected together and engaged in a vast plot to convince the individual that things are normal.

Interestingly, in the 'big con' in which a whole social establishment may be put together to provide a few minutes of convincing background display, the mark is, in fact, as much the center of the design as any potentate could wish for, but, of course, the connectedness is only covert; if the operators are to succeed, they must convince the mark that he is but an incidental user of the place and that all the other individuals and artifacts have a reason to be there independent of him, being involved in projects of action independent of his, that, in brief, they are merely alongside him.[2]

Now in everyday life it is highly unlikely that any individual will be faced with such elaborate contrivances, but in virtually any situation in which we find ourselves it is at least possible that this is happening. Even when everything appears to be perfectly normal and as it should be, it is possible that everything is in fact contrived. It may be more likely for us to find ourselves in situations where certain, perhaps relatively small, though nevertheless significant, features are contrived. Thus, the house that is offered for sale to the prospective owner-occupier is certainly not a contrived illusion, but the impression that he gains that it is free from rising damp and structural defects may well be such, achieved by the judicious filling of cracks and use of foil paper to conceal damp patches, all covered over by inconspicuous redecoration. If things are contrived, those responsible for the contrivance are likely to do all they can to ensure that things appear to be normal to their victim. Some people, such as policemen and security guards, may have special responsibilities to maintain an alertness for the possibility of contrivances, but ordinarily, people are not expected to suspect continually that the situations they find themselves in are contrived, and those who persist in doing so may well be regarded as paranoic and placed in mental hospitals. There are, however, some quite ordinary situations where it may be wise for people to be wary of contrivances. The house hunter, as our earlier example suggests, is wise to be wary of new wallpaper in old houses, and the prospective second-hand car purchaser may be wise to consider whether the quiet and healthy sounds of the car do not reflect the use of thick oil in the engine and sawdust in the gearbox, rather than mechanical perfection. In demonstrating the bizarre possibilities that can be entertained when situations are not taken at their face value, Goffman's work helps us to understand the social pressures on the individual to take for granted that things are what they seem.

Some sociologists have attempted to examine the process involved in the individual's construction of his definition of the situation by placing people experimentally in situations in which the cues that might be relied on for defining the situation are disordered.[3] Such experiments are rather like the confidence trick in reverse, for whereas the confidence trickster manipulates the scene to ensure that appearances are normal, in this case the experimenter contrives things to ensure that things do not appear as normal. The point of such experiments is to enable the sociologist to observe the individual checking the components of his definition of the situation in the face of inconsistencies. Peter McHugh has described two general elements of the definition of the situation: relativity and emergence.[4] *Relativity* refers to our assumptions concerning the spatial relationship between those elements present in the situation. In the doctor's surgery, we assume that the complex technological equipment surrounding us is apparatus used in the course of medical practice, even if we are not sure just exactly what purposes some of the equipment serves. If we become suspicious, and start to question our taken-for-granted assumptions, the possibilities may emerge that the equipment is connected not with the practice of medicine but with forgery or espionage: more bizarrely, it might even be possible that the equipment is designed for extracting information by means of torture from victims who have been unsuspectingly lured into the situation. For our individual in the street who is victim of the 'big con', he assumes that the activities of everyone he observes are connected only in a somewhat random and coincidental fashion, whereas they are in fact very closely co-ordinated as part of a grand design.

Emergence refers to the temporal element in the definition of the situation, the significance of the situation in relation to the past and the future.* The definition of a present situation depends upon our understanding of significant events preceding the situation, and the consequences of the situation for future events. Thus, the definition of an encounter between two people depends upon their understanding of relevant aspects of each other's biography, including their past relationship, and their expectations of future outcomes of their encounter. Whether or not one knows a person one encounters, what one knows of him, and whether and in what circumstances one is likely to meet him again, all influence the definition of the situation. Thus, social survey interviewers often find the people they interview to be exceptionally frank about intimate personal matters. This is because people are often willing to reveal such matters to strangers in the knowledge that they are unlikely to meet them ever again. The past, the present and the future are closely interrelated, continually changing and modifying each other. For those engaged in laborious and monotonous manual work, the definition of the situation will be quite different according to whether those engaged in such work are engaged temporarily, on vacation as students, or whether they expect to continue in such work for years ahead. Experiences of the present

---

* This usage should not be confused with the philosophical concept of emergence, which is quite different.

and new expectations for the future may result in redefinitions of the past. Thus, the soldier may redefine a battlefield encounter if he subsequently learns that he is to be awarded a medal for it, and perhaps redefine it rather differently if he learns that he is to be courtmartialled for it instead. Escapades and practical jokes will be redefined if they produce unfortunate outcomes. A chance meeting between two people at a bus-stop may go through several stages of redefinition if those people subsequently get married.

If we suspect, finding ourselves in a given situation, that things are other than what they seem, then we may begin to examine our taken-for-granted assumptions about the past and the future in relation to the present situation. Thus, we assume that the doctor treating us in his surgery has arrived in the present situation as a result of undergoing proper medical training and a more or less normal medical career. If we doubt whether things are what they seem, then we may wonder whether the doctor is a real doctor, and whether, therefore, it may not be a rather different series of past events that has led him into the present situation; perhaps training in techniques of espionage and counter-intelligence, rather than medical training. In this case, doubts about the present lead us to review our taken-for-granted assumptions about the past. If in the course of a taxi ride we are led to doubt whether it is really a taxi that we are travelling in, and, therefore, whether the driver is really a taxi-driver, we may proceed to review our assumptions about where the taxi is taking us. Here, doubts about the present lead us to review our taken-for-granted expectations about the future. McHugh suggests that when doubts arise over the ordering of a situation it is usually the assumptions of relativity, the relations between elements of the current situation, that are brought into question first: these in turn lead to a review of assumptions of emergence.[5]

The examples given to illustrate the procedures in defining the situation have been rather sensational and bizarre. Yet in ordinary everyday life our assumptions and the procedures whereby the situation is defined may be rarely thrown into question and thus usually unnoticed. The focus on the sensational and bizarre is necessary to direct our attention to these procedures and assumptions.

The significance of W. I. Thomas's famous statement: 'If men define situations as real, then they are real in their consequences', lies in the fact that people's actions are dependent upon the way they define their situations. People respond to what they see to be the reality of their situation, and it may not make much difference whether or not their perception is accurate. If, for example, the police define a situation as a riot, it may make little difference to subsequent events whether or not their definition was in accordance with that of an 'objective' observer. Robert K. Merton has shown how Thomas's theory can be used to explain self-fulfilling prophecies.[6] People believe that a bank is about to collapse financially, and therefore rush to retrieve their deposits. The run on the bank, caused only by the belief in the bank's imminent insolvency, ensures that the bank does in fact collapse. 'C'-stream children may be defined by their teachers as lacking in ability, capacity for work and other virtuous qualities, and as they become aware of this definition of themselves, their behaviour is likely to be in accordance with it. According to Merton, the self-fulfilling prophecy is 'in the beginning, a *false* definition evoking a new behaviour which makes the originally false conception come *true*'.[7] However, such a neat distinction between true and false definitions may be difficult to apply in practice. It may be reassuring for the sociologist to believe that he is able to assess the truth or falsity of definitions of the situation by comparing his own 'objective' assessment with the 'subjective' definitions of the participants in the situation, but this may be a mistaken and misleading belief. The objectivity of sociology lies not in that it attempts an 'objective' appraisal of social reality to replace common-sense 'subjective' theories and perspectives, but rather in its attempt to define social reality through the analysis and understanding of the way people construct their social worlds. This is why the 'definition of the situation' is an important sociological concept. The superiority of sociological knowledge over everyday common-sense knowledge of the social world is dependent upon the sociologist's endeavour to encompass and go beyond everyday definitions of the social world. However, it could be argued that in the end we still have only conflicting definitions of the situation: that there is no absolute objective standard of social reality against which we can measure the way people define the social world.

In emphasising the subjective nature of definitions of the situation, and in challenging the notion of the 'objective' view of the scientist or detached observer, we have introduced the idea that social reality is always socially defined, and is always understood in terms of subjective, if shared, definitions of the situation. Definitions are always subjective, and thus the distinction between 'subjective' and 'objective' interpretations of reality, the 'inside' and 'outside' points of view, is at best only

relative, and, at worst, misleading. The contrast between the objective
appraisal of a situation by an outside investigator, and the subjective
definition of those involved in the situation is, if these do conflict,
rather a contrast between conflicting subjective definitions – conflicting
because they are derived from different points of view, different perspectives. This does pose some rather serious difficulties if we are to
maintain any claim for the objectivity of sociology, difficulties which
will be considered in the concluding chapter of this book. If social
reality is socially constructed, then perhaps the notion that 'if men
define situations as real, they are real in their consequences' could be
shortened to read 'if men define situations as real, they are real'. The
reality of society exists in so far as it is experienced by its members. As
the early American sociologist Charles Cooley once wrote: 'the
imaginations which people have of one another are the solid facts of
society'.[8]

Such extreme subjectivist views raise a number of philosophical
problems with which we cannot be concerned here, though this is not
to say they are not the concern of sociologists. Sociological problems
are raised too, which must be attended to. If people believe that their
society provides equal educational opportunity for all, does this mean
there is in fact equal educational opportunity for all? If a survey
discloses that the majority of people in a society believe that there are
no social classes, should the sociologist conclude that the society is
therefore classless? Such beliefs may be real enough in their consequences, but it would hardly seem sensible to suggest that people are
not sometimes clearly mistaken in their interpretations of situations.
It has already been noted that people may arrive at quite inappropriate
definitions of the situation as a result of the contrivances of others.
Furthermore, mistaken, or false definitions of the situation may occur
when those who hold them are either deprived of, or choose to ignore,
available information which would render their definitions incompatible with the procedures whereby they construct social reality. Many
people in Britain today might believe that poverty is a result of un-
willingness or inability to work, or at least occurs mainly in families
where the father is not in regular full-time work. Such people might
recognise that they are mistaken if they learn that many thousands of
families in which the father is in full-time work do live at a level which
they would define as poverty. The subjectivist viewpoint, regarding
social reality as a social construction, is a valuable corrective to the
tendency to see neat 'subjective' and 'objective' views of the social

order, but should not be embraced to the extent that we are unable to recognise some definitions of the situation as mistaken, false, or wrong. It is anyway the task of the sociologist to subject to his analysis the taken-for-granted definitions of social reality, and not to take them for granted himself.

One reason for the difficulty of making distinctions between true and false definitions of the situation is that definitions may include moral and factual elements which are not clearly discernible. Our discussion of moral and factual expectations in the previous chapter suggested that these are not neat discrete categories. Our expectations of what will be and what ought to be are not always clearly distinguished, and much the same could be said of definitions of the situation: definitions of the situation are always likely to be influenced by social norms. Some definitions may be clearly moral, in which case standards of truth and falsity are not in any event applicable. The definition, for example, of a publication as obscene would be such a moral definition: obscenity implies offensiveness, and if it is taken, as it is in English legal fiction, to imply tendencies to deprave and corrupt, then it may be said that notions of depravity and corruption are moral notions. Often, however, purportedly factual definitions may turn out to be moral definitions in disguise. It may seem, for example, that it would be possible to show the white racialist that his definition of blacks as inferior could be changed by indicating that it was not substantiated by reasonable, scientific evidence. But the racialist, even if he accepts the evidence, may always find escape clauses, perhaps switching the basis for his invidious distinction from measurable abilities to more obscure qualities. Reasonable, scientific evidence alone does not destroy the racialist definition because it is basically a moral (or, as I would prefer, immoral) definition: the invidious distinction between groups of people on the basis of skin colour represents the world both as it is and as it ought to be.

Definitions of the situation and the moral order of social life are thus closely linked to one another. Chapter 2 concluded with the suggestion that the maintenance of social norms and changes in the normative order must be seen in terms of the distribution of power in society: powerful groups are in stronger positions to influence social norms than powerless ones. Similarly, the extent to which certain definitions of the situation in society are shared may depend on the distribution of power in society. Powerful people are able to persuade others to accept their definition of the situation, and that the definitions of 'experts' are

authoritative may not be unconnected with the approval and acceptance of the given 'expertise' by the powerful. It is thus possible to link
the concept of definition of the situation to the perspective of power
and conflict. To a degree, the sociologist is forced to adopt a radical
standpoint in so far as his analysis penetrates the authoritative and
established definitions of social reality.

The subjectivist view presents for us the reality of social life as the
interpretations and imaginations of social life for its participants. But
these definitions, interpretations and imaginations are themselves a
product of social life, and of the distribution of power in social life.
A conceptual link is needed to relate the individual's definition of the
situation to the structure of society.

REFERENCE GROUPS AND THE GENERALISED OTHER

The concept of reference group enables us to see how the individual's
definition of the situation is a product of his participation in social life.
It is his own subjective construction, but, as we have already suggested,
social life is very dependent upon its members sharing definitions of
the situation. In formulating his own definition of the situation, the
individual will take into account, and be influenced by, his perception
of how others might define the situation. The suburbanite's assessment
of his garden with its profusion of wild flowers will not be unaffected
by the way he sees that others, perhaps his neighbours, will assess it,
regarding its neglect with guilt and depressed by the thought of the
labour required to improve it. However, were the suburbanite to be a
botanist, and the wild flowers around his house to include very rare
species likely to be destroyed by any cultivation, his definition of the
situation would be very different, influenced more by the perception
of how the situation would be defined by other botanists than by the
neighbours.

The way in which other people's definition of the situation might
influence our own is quite varied. The walking enthusiast may be well
aware of people who would define his plodding in the rain through
moorland bogs as a singularly unpleasant activity, but it may not in the
least affect his conception of his activity as enjoyable recreation. Those
'others' are not significant others for him in this situation, and in the
given situation he is indifferent to them (though some of them,
perhaps including work mates, may be highly significant others in
different situations). Sometimes, our own definition of the situation
may be reinforced by our awareness of contradictory definitions by

some others. The *avant-garde* enthusiast's enjoyment of a piece of esoteric music may in part depend upon his recognition that uninitiated and ignorant masses regard such music as a series of tedious or painful noises. The teenage rebel's enjoyment of illicit activities may be enhanced by his knowledge that the 'authorities' define them as mindless vandalism. He is not indifferent to the 'authorities': they are still significant others for him in the situation, but their significance is negative.

To say that the individual's definition of the situation is influenced by how he perceives others would define the situation does not mean that these others are always concrete, specific individuals. As our last example illustrates, these 'others' may sometimes be highly generalised: the 'authorities' is a highly generalised and vague category, but in the situation a specific corporate view may be attached to it. At an even more general level, we may sometimes be influenced by how we would imagine 'people in general' would define the situation. Our ideas about 'people in general' correspond to the social psychological concept of the 'generalised other', developed by the American social psychologist and philosopher, George Herbert Mead. For Mead, 'the attitude of the generalised other is the attitude of the whole community'.[9] He gives as an example a team ball-game, in which members of the team experience the team itself as the generalised other. Each team member, rather than work out the individual definitions and expectations of every other member of the team impinging upon him, can treat the team as a generalised category: the team has its definitions, and its expectations. The generalised other may be conceived of as the influence of 'society' upon the individual, the individual's conception of society's expectations, society's definition of the situation, but it may also be seen as referring to more specific and limited groups of people – people in this particular local community, one's particular profession, young people, football fans, students, Christians, and so on. In each case, the individual focuses on the attitudes, definitions and expectations not of specific concrete individuals, but on those of generalised social groups.

The significance of such generalised others for the individual lies in that it is by reference to these others that he defines his situation. In defining the situation, the individual chooses to adopt the standpoint of selected generalised others, to see the situation as a scholar, a respectable citizen, or a socialist would see it. Mead makes the following comments on the influence of the generalised other:

It is in the form of the generalised other that the social process influences the behaviour of the individuals involved in it and carrying it on, i.e., that the community exercises control over the conduct of its individual members; for it is in this form that the social process or community enters as a determining factor into the individual's thinking.[10]

Generalised others that are significant for the individual – those that influence his definition of the situation – may be conceived as reference groups. The concept of 'reference group' has occupied a central place in sociological theories of social interaction and social psychology since the 1940s, but it would be neither possible nor desirable here to attempt to review the various ways in which the concept has been employed. Perhaps one of the most useful definitions to emerge, and one that is consistent with the approach adopted here, is that offered by Shibutani, who defines a reference group as 'that group whose presumed perspective is used by an actor as the frame of reference in the organisation of his perceptual field'.[11] In defining the situation, the individual adopts the perspective of one or more reference groups: the individual's perspective on social reality is dependent upon his reference groups, and, indeed, it may be said that without reference groups the individual has no basis for the ordering of social reality. The concept of reference group is sometimes used to include all the 'others' who may influence the individual's definition of the situation, so that it may refer to a single person as well as to social groups. While this may be useful for social psychologists, the concern here is with *social*, not interpersonal, influences on the individual's construction of his social world. For the sociologist, the reference group is a social group, referring to generalised rather than specific others. As Ralph Turner suggests, 'The reference group is a generalised other viewed as possessing member roles and attributes independently of the specific individuals who compose it.'[12]

Yet if the reference group is a social group, it is a social group only in a rather special sense: it is a social group only in the mind of the individual who employs it. Reference groups confront the individual as objective, external social groups – the working class, people over thirty, the 'authorities', socialists – but the perspectives and standpoints of these social groups are subjectively interpreted by the individual: as Shibutani's definition suggests, it is the *presumed* perspective of the group that influences the individual. Reference groups represent social influences on the individual's definition of the situation and thereby his actions, but only in so far as they are interpreted and understood by the individual. Sometimes it is suggested that reference groups may be real or imaginary social groups, that an individual's reference group may or may not be a representation of a real social group. Thus, the community of a church as a reference group would represent a real social group, whereas a community of saints might represent an imaginary one. From this example, the distinction might appear to be quite clear, and it does serve to reinforce the point that reference groups need not be concrete social groups. Yet it is not so clear when we consider the question of how far an individual's interpretation of a reference group which does have some empirical referent is a real or imaginary one. Is the academic's conception of the academic profession as a reference group, or the worker's conception of managers, real or imaginary? It may be misleading and inappropriate to ask these questions, because whether an individual's interpretation of the standpoint of a social group is real or imaginary may turn out to be a question of whether his interpretation is the one he *ought* to have. The bank clerk may perceive bank managers as people not engaged in 'real work' because they spend much of their time just talking to people, rather than filling out forms, counting money, or operating machines. But if it is said that this is an imaginary rather than real view of the work of bank managers, the implication may be not so much that it is a factually inaccurate view, but rather that this is not the way managers ought to be regarded: the time spent by the manager talking to people, even at the golf club, *ought* to be seen as real work. In other words, practical distinctions between reference groups which are real and imaginary may, at least in part, be moral rather than factual distinctions. This is not to say that conceptions of reference groups may not misrepresent social groups and that the sociologist should not analyse such misrepresentations: as noted in the preceding section, it would be foolish not to allow that people's definition of the situation may be mistaken. The concept of reference group is, however, a subjective concept, and the reality of a social group as a reference group lies in the experience and understanding of it by the individual adopting it as a reference group. The social reality of social groups as reference groups lies in that such experiences and understandings are shared. We are brought back to the proposition that if men define situations as real, they are real in their consequences.

NORMATIVE AND COMPARATIVE REFERENCE GROUPS

Sociologists often distinguish between different types of reference groups, the commonest distinction being that between 'normative' and 'comparative' reference groups.[13] The 'membership' reference group is also sometimes conceived as a distinct type.

While it is not the intention here to dwell on definitions and classifications of concepts, these distinctions are valuable for the understanding of the social processes whereby reference groups influence social action: it is primarily for these reasons that they were devised. It will be apparent that the distinctions are not altogether satisfactory, but their limitations and inadequacies serve to draw attention to aspects of reference groups that might otherwise escape us.

'Normative' reference groups are defined as those groups from which the individual takes his normative or moral standards. It is by reference to these groups that he defines the moral element in the situation. Observing social activities at a party, the guest may define them as moral or immoral conduct according to his 'normative' reference groups. If these groups include puritanical religious groups endorsing severe sexual repression, then we might expect him to regard the observed activities, and the very fact that he is present to observe such activities, as immoral.

'Comparative' reference groups are those groups which provide the individual with a frame of reference for evaluating his own social position relative to others. A village school headmaster may regard his position as one of distinction if his reference group is the local village community. On the other hand, if his reference group is what he regards as the élite of the teaching profession – headmasters of large urban schools – then he may regard his position as one of relative failure and obscurity. The use by the individual of comparative reference groups would seem to presuppose an initial ordering of social life as in some sense hierarchical. If the particular choice of 'comparative' reference groups indicates the criteria of defining the pecking order and the individual's relative position within it, the use of comparative reference groups at all depends upon a prior frame of reference ordering social life on some hierarchical basis. Thus, the use of 'comparative' reference groups presupposes the recognition of social inequality.

'Membership' reference groups refer to those groups of which the individual regards himself as a member. It is one of the basic postulates of interaction theorists that the individual experiences himself through his understanding of the perception of others. Thus, the individual's 'membership' groups in a sense give him his identity: he is a loving husband, a respectable citizen, a good clubman, a manager, middle class, conservative and Christian. Each component of this identity refers to groups of people perceived as generalised others. All the individual's reference groups may be seen as either 'membership' or 'non-membership' groups. Robert K. Merton has suggested that one of the major tasks of reference group theory is the analysis of the conditions under which membership groups provide the individual's frame of reference, and those under which non-membership groups provide the frame of reference.[14] 'Membership' groups provide the basis for the perception of 'non-membership' groups as comparative groups, though, as pointed out by Runciman,[15] comparative groups are in a sense membership groups in that comparison depends upon the recognition of at least some common attributes. A local Labour Party compares its fortunes with the local Conservative Party, because both share membership of the local political community. 'Membership' reference groups, it should be clear, do not refer to concrete social groups in which people participate, but to the perceived generalised others with which the individual identifies.

The types of reference groups described show how they may define for the individual his moral standards, his evaluation of his social position, and his identity. A more detailed examination of these types provides some indication of the social processes that can be described in terms of reference groups.

First, it may be useful to make some further comments on the distinction between comparative and normative reference groups. They are distinct in the sense that social positions are compared, positively or negatively, as favourable or unfavourable, whereas norms are adopted or rejected, and are not subject to comparisons. An individual may regard his social position as inferior to those of others, but he cannot regard his norms as such, because his norms provide his standards of moral conduct, and in terms of them other norms are inappropriate. The deferential hotel waiter may regard those he attends as his social superiors, but unless he adopts their norms they are inappropriate for him: thus the 'refined' speech and etiquette of the waiter may be revealed as stage-managed performances and a subject for amusement once the kitchen door is closed. However, the distinction may be misleading if it is taken to mean that only normative reference groups refer to norms and that comparative groups refer only to the material conditions of social life. Comparative reference groups are bases for evaluations: comparisons are made in terms of attributes that are valued, whether they may be material wealth, physical attributes, or particular skills and abilities. The assessment of comparative reference groups is thus both moral and factual, and the very choice of comparative reference groups is a moral choice: certain groups ought to serve as a frame of reference, others ought not.

RELATIVE DEPRIVATION

The notion of relative deprivation is an important and valuable concept that is closely associated with comparative reference groups, and also points to the significance of the normative basis of comparative reference groups. Deprivation is felt, it may be said, when people are aware that their conditions of life are lacking in some aspects, aspects which they see that groups of other people enjoy, and which they feel that they themselves ought to have. Relative deprivation refers to deprivation felt with reference to specific groups of, or generalised, others: it is, in other words, determined by the individual's choice of comparative reference groups. Whether or not the manual worker whose income and conditions of work are much inferior to those of professional workers feels deprived, in relation to professional workers, depends upon whether or not the professional groups serve as a comparative reference group for him. It is not simply that people feel deprived when they are able to observe others enjoying desired goods which they themselves do not have. They must, in addition, feel that they too ought to be able to enjoy such goods. Relative deprivation implies both perceived social inequality and perceived social injustice. Peasants in a feudal village may be only too well aware of the differences between their own situation and the splendour of the local feudal lord, but they may have learnt to regard this as right and proper and hence not feel relatively deprived. Often, however, and less obviously, social research has shown that people are remarkably unaware of the extent of social inequalities in their own society. In his study of relative deprivation and social inequality in Britain, W. G. Runciman found a very limited amount of relative deprivation in relation to social inequality among manual workers, and he saw this in terms of their limited range of comparative reference groups: manual workers were likely to limit their comparative reference groups to other groups of manual workers. These are some of the replies he received to the question: 'Do you think there are any other sorts of people doing noticeably better at the moment than you and your family?':

> 'People with no children', said a woman with four of them. 'Where there is a man working in the family', said an unmarried woman. 'People who get extra money by letting off part of the house', said an 82-year-old widow. . . . 'People that have good health and are able to be in full time work', said a retired draper. 'People on night work', said a 63-year-old brazier in the engineering industry, 'I have now had to do day work – I'm getting old'.[16]

These answers illustrate how people's comparative reference groups are limited by the range of their social experience. A more recent sociological study of a poor district of Nottingham, undertaken by Ken Coates and Richard Silburn, illustrates how limited are the conceptions of 'wealth' held by poor people.

> In October 1966, at the time of our first survey, the average weekly wage of an adult man was £20 6s. od. Taking a sum a little less than £5 more than this for convenience, we estimate that one household in every six we interviewed thought that £25 (in some cases even a smaller sum) was 'wealth' and of those who could suggest a figure at all nearly three-quarters chose a sum no greater than £50 a week. It is safe to say that a large proportion of the people in St Ann's regard as riches (beyond the dreams of their avarice at any rate) an income which many middle-class people would think as penury.[17]

The people of St Ann's have limited conceptions of wealth because of their restricted comparative reference groups. Both the studies cited make the point that while everyone knows that people such as pop singers, film stars and industrial tycoons have enormous incomes, such figures are rarely adopted as comparative reference groups. For ordinary people, they are not part of the real, everyday, concrete world, but rather a part of a glamorous, semi-fantasy world, experienced only through the cinema and television screen.

The significance of comparative reference groups, then, is revealed in the concept of relative deprivation, with its implications for the analysis of social inequality, poverty and social justice. Normative reference groups, as groups from which the individual takes his normative or moral standards, are of particular significance in terms of deviance and marginality.

DEVIANCE AND MARGINALITY

Deviance is dealt with at length in Chapter 5 and the concern here is solely to indicate the relevance of the notion of normative reference groups to it. Deviance may be simply and rather crudely defined as non-conformity to social norms. If we consider that in any society different social groups may hold somewhat different social norms, then we may see the deviant more specifically as an individual who deviates from the social norms of the groups in which he participates.

It must be noted that certain social groups, such as hippie communards, professional criminals, and gypsies, while possessing their own sets of social norms, may be regarded as deviant in terms of wider societal norms. The relevance of the concept of the normative reference group to deviance is that it suggests a substantial modification of the simple view of the deviant as someone who deviates or fails to live up to given norms. Our sociological perspective suggests that normative reference groups are not merely groups or conceptions which occasionally influence people's activities in their more moral moments, representing a sort of sociological conscience which occasionally pricks us. The pervasiveness of the moral order of social life was shown in Chapter 2, and here we may see normative reference groups as universal in application, regulating social behaviour in general. In this light, the deviant is not someone who does not adhere to social norms, but rather someone who adheres to the wrong ones – norms which are other than those held by those social groups in which he participates. In other words, the deviant is choosing a different set of normative reference groups from those of his fellows, reference groups which from the point of view of his fellows are inappropriate. As the American philosopher Thoreau once put it, 'If a man does not keep pace with his companions, perhaps it is because he hears a different drummer.' The deviant is not simply a non-conformist, but someone who conforms to a set of standards rather different from those of most other people. The delinquent boy who conforms to the norms of his peer group rather than those of his teachers is a commonplace in sociological literature. The teacher who uses his teaching for the purposes of political indoctrination and recruitment may be a deviant who in his teaching situation takes his political party as his normative reference group rather than his profession. Yet in seeing normative reference groups as all-pervasive, it must be remembered that while they confront the individuals who choose them as objective, external social groups, they are in fact subjectively defined, and indeed, deviance may follow from rather unusual, or deviant, subjective perceptions of normative reference groups. The aspiring amateur and would-be professional actor who behaves histrionically and flamboyantly in the theatre bar has a conception of professional actors as a reference group which is somewhat different from the conception held by professional actors themselves, who generally reserve their histrionics for the stage. That deviance may follow from deviant conceptions of reference groups indicates that the notion of the normative reference group does not in any sense provide an explanation of deviance. It does, however, provide a corrective to a simple conformity/non-conformity view of deviance, and serves to focus on deviance from the point of view of the deviant.

The normative reference group concept, then, suggests a view of the deviant as an individual whose normative reference groups are other than those of the social groups to which he belongs. A special case of such deviance is the individual who adopts the norms of a social group in order to be admitted to this group, even though the norms which he now adopts are in opposition to those of the group of which he is currently a member. R. K. Merton has discussed this process as anticipatory socialisation.[18] Analysing material from *The American Soldier*,[19] Merton discusses the case of enlisted men who seek promotion to the officer corps. These men may proceed by adhering strictly to the official army norms, which are in fact the norms approved by the officers, but not approved by other enlisted men. The aspiring soldiers will be regarded as 'boot-lickers' and 'suckers' by their fellows. Those of them who fail to gain promotion despite these efforts will end up rejected by both the officer corps and their fellow enlisted men.

Their anticipatory socialisation has failed, and they are marginal men. Marginal people thus are those who, in aspiring to move from one social group to another, end up by being rejected by both.

A rather delightful depiction of marginality is given by Anthony Trollope in his novel *Barchester Towers*. At a garden party given by the squire, the gentry are entertained in the house and on the lawn, while the lower orders – the tenant farmers and labourers and their families – are accommodated in a tent in the paddock. One tenant farmer's wife, a Mrs Lookaloft, who has adopted many of the fashions of the gentry and sends her children to boarding school, pushes herself uninvited into the circle of the gentry.

Mrs Lookaloft had no business there . . . she was not wanted there, and would not be welcome. But he [the footman] had not the courage to tell a stout lady with a low dress, short sleeves and satin at eight shillings a yard, that she had come to the wrong tent: . . . And thus Mrs Lookaloft carried her point, broke through the guards, and made her way into the citadel. That she would have to pass an uncomfortable time there she had surmised before. But nothing now could rob her of the power of boasting that she had consorted on the lawn with the squire and Miss Thorne, with a countess, a bishop and the country grandees, while Mrs Greenacre and such like were walking about with the ploughboys in the park.[20]

The news of Mrs Lookaloft shortly reached the paddock:

'I do tell 'ee plainly – face to face – she be there in madam's drawing room; herself and Gussy, and them two walloping gals, dressed up to their very eyeses'. This was said by a very positive, very indignant, and very fat farmer's wife. . . .[21]

Marginal people are usually unsuccessful would-be social climbers, though they may not be. The radical middle-class intellectual who identifies with the working class, consciously adopts a working-class style of life and attempts to participate in working-class social life, but is not accepted by working-class social groups, is also a marginal man.

The concept of reference group thus gives us much insight into the social processes involved in defining the situation, and is useful for the understanding of such phenomena as relative deprivation, deviance and marginality. So far, however, the focus has been upon the individual's definition of the elements of the situation in relation to himself, rather than on the definition of himself in relation to other elements of his situation. The notion of 'membership' reference group is useful for considering the individual's definition of himself: he sees himself as a member of particular groups – respectable good citizens, ordinary people, professional people, and so on – and may adopt the perceived norms of these groups. But we cannot go very far with this sort of analysis without introducing the concept of role. It is only through the concept of role that we are able to comprehend the individual as active, as a social actor, rather than, as our emphasis has been so far, as an interpreter of social reality.

4. Role Playing

The sociologist's idea of man in society is encapsulated in the concept of role. For the sociologist, man is seen as a player of his social roles, his roles as businessman, husband, father, golfer, community leader and churchman, or as fitter, shop steward, husband, father, party-worker and bowls player.

THE DEFINITION OF ROLES

In Chapter 2, normative expectations were described as subjective counterparts to norms. When individuals occupy particular positions, they find that each position they occupy subjects them to particular expectations from their fellows. In one's occupational roles, one is expected to perform the tasks associated with these roles in the pre-scribed manner, and in one's family roles, one is expected to undertake one's familial duties. A role may therefore be defined, following Gross, Mason and McEachern,[1] as a set of expectations impinging upon an individual occupying a social position. Expectations are counterparts to social norms, and so it may be said that roles are defined by the norms of society: we are required to do what 'society' expects of us in our occupational, familial and other roles. Sociologists sometimes describe roles in terms of what society expects and demands. Thus, Talcott Parsons contrasts what society expects of the medical practi-tioner with what is expected of businessmen in American society.

[It is] the pattern of the business world [that] . . . each party to the situation is expected to be orientated to the rational pursuit of his own self interests, and where there is an approach to the idea of 'caveat emptor'. In a broad sense it is surely clear that society would not tolerate the privileges which have been vested in the medical profession on such terms. . . . it is noteworthy how strongly the main reliance for control is placed on 'informal' mechanisms. The law of the state includes severe penalties for 'malpractice' and medical associations have relatively elaborate disciplinary procedures, but these are not the principal mechanisms which operate to ensure the control of self-orientation tendencies.

> [The physician] cannot advertise – he can only modestly announce by his shingle and the use of his M.D. in telephone directories and classified sections that he is able to provide medical service. He cannot bargain over fees with his patients – a 'take it or leave it' attitude is enjoined upon him. He cannot refuse patients on the grounds that they are poor 'credit risks'. He is given the privilege of charging according to the 'sliding scale', that is, in proportion to the income of the patient or his family – a drastic difference from the usual pricing mechanism of the business world.[2]

Roles involve two kinds of expectations, the expectations 'society' has of the role player, the role player's obligations, and the expectations the role player has of 'society' or of others with whom he interacts in playing his role, his rights. Thus Parsons, in the above quotation, notes that the medical practitioner has privileges in return for his obligation to conduct his practice on principles rather different from those of business. It is unnecessary to elaborate upon the fact that the marital partner has both rights and obligations in the role of spouse.

The idea of roles as sets of expectations imposed by 'society' upon the holders of social positions is consistent with the perspective of 'society' presented in Chapter 1. There, it was pointed out that this perspective implied that the individuals fitted into the roles set out for them by society. In this view, roles may be seen as part of the structure of society, the occupational, family, authority and other roles which 'society' lays out for people to attach themselves to. Indeed, the structure of society may be seen as interrelated patterns of roles. Yet while roles are part of the structure of society, they exist only in so far as they are filled by individuals. In the end, there are only individual husbands, teachers, and policemen. Generalised conceptions of the roles of husband, teacher and policeman exist only in abstraction. The role concept may thus be seen to provide a fundamental link between the structure of society and the individual. The perspective of 'society' is a determinist perspective, and the view of role as expectations imposed by society is itself determinist. Later in this chapter, this view will be counterbalanced with a conception of role derived from the individualistic perspective, presenting a voluntaristic view of the role player as active and creative. Combining these perspectives in the analysis of role furthers our understanding of the relationship between the individual and society and the tensions and conflicts that this contains.

It is first necessary to ask just how it is that 'society' imposes its expectations upon role players. Following Dahrendorf,[3] it may be noted that role expectations derive from social norms, and that the individual orientates to social norms by means of his normative reference groups. As has been pointed out in Chapter 3 (p. 66), the individual's reference groups are those significant generalised others whose perspectives the individual takes into account in defining his situation. Normative reference groups, as defined in Chapter 3 (p. 68), are those reference groups from which the individual takes the norms governing his behaviour, and it is from these also that he takes the expectations impinging upon his roles, his rights and obligations in the roles he plays. Thus, the role of teacher may be defined in terms of the expectations of pupils, parents, educational administrators, teachers and other groups that are significant for the teacher's role as generalised others. Each of these groups serves as a reference group for the teacher, and he takes into account their expectations in the performance of his role.

A somewhat different answer to the question as to who defines society's expectations of the role player is given by Gross, Mason and McEachern in their study of school superintendents in America,[4] though superficially the approach adopted by them might seem to be identical. The role of school superintendent is seen as defined by the expectations of other role players whose roles are structurally related to the school superintendent's role. Thus the school superintendent's role is defined by teachers, parents, pupils, local government officers and elected representatives in local government: the expectations of all these people must be taken into account by school superintendents in the course of their work. To analyse how these expectations impinge upon school superintendents, the authors of the study suggest that we should see the role of school superintendent as composed of a number of sectors, each sector comprising the expectations of one particular group with whom the superintendent has relationships in the course of his work. Thus, one sector would be derived from the relation of the superintendent with teachers, another from his relations with local government officers, and yet another from his relations with other school superintendents in other districts. The different groups of people may have different and sometimes conflicting expectations of the school superintendent, as the authors discovered in the course of their research. Thus, the idea of conceiving role as a set of role sectors is useful in analysing role conflict, as will be seen below.

The difference between the two approaches outlined above lies in that while Dahrendorf sees roles defined in terms of reference groups, for Gross, Mason and McEachern, role expectations are defined by actual concrete groups and individuals. Reference groups, it will be recalled, refer to generalised others, not to concrete social groups and individuals. Dahrendorf argues that to treat role expectations as deriving from particular, concrete groups and individuals results in the mistaken view that the roles we play simply derive from the opinions of those with whom we interact, and criticises Gross, Mason and McEachern for giving this impression.

> If six out of ten parents interviewed think that a school superinten-
> dent should not smoke or be married, these attributes or actions are
> for Gross constituents of the role of school superintendent; if, on
> the other hand – Gross does not go this far, but nothing in his
> approach rules out such absurdities – thirty-five out of forty pupils
> think that none of them should ever get bad marks, this too is an
> expectation, associated in the first instance with the role of teacher
> but applying also to the school superintendent as the teacher's
> superior.[5]

His point is that role expectations derive from social norms, which are not the same thing as opinions. Thus, the teacher may be aware that there is some difference between what 3C would like him to do and his conception of the expectations of pupils as generalised others, though this latter conception may well be coloured by the behaviour of 3C. Furthermore, pupils in 3C may distinguish between what they would like their teacher to do and what he ought to do to be judged by them to be a good teacher. They may, for instance, be quite pleased that he never looks at any of their written work, because this means that they never have to do any proper work, but at the same time they may be aware that this is hardly the mark of a good teacher. The relationships between norms and opinions are complex, but at least I hope to have illustrated the point that they are not the same.

Dahrendorf, in separating role expectations from individual opinions, emphasises the determinist perspective of society. But with the employment of the concept of reference group, the individualistic perspective creeps in. Reference groups, as was pointed out in Chapter 3 (p. 66), are subjectively defined, and thus the teacher, in orientating his behaviour to the expectations of pupils, parents and superiors, is behaving according to what he, the individual teacher, perceives to be the expectations of these groups as generalised others.

In Chapter 2 (p. 52), the point was made that individual expectations that are inconsistent with social norms may lead to modifications and changes in the norms. Similarly, the individual's perceptions of the expectations of his reference groups will be modified in the light of his experience of the personal representatives of these groups. This point will be taken up later (pp. 85–6) in a discussion of innovation in role playing, where it will be seen that the varying expectations of the particular people a role player interacts with are of considerable significance for his role performance.

It is now perhaps worth while to consider the conception of sociological man as a player of social roles emerging from the discussion so far. Any one individual fills a number of roles at any one time, for at the very least he is likely to perform occupational, family and leisure roles, and possibly many more. So we have a picture of each individual segmented by the sociologist into a number of roles, each of which is further compartmentalised into a number of role sectors. By such compartmentalisation, it may seem that the sociologist loses sight of the person, and thereby drains all humanity out of the people he studies. This may sometimes happen, but it is not inherent in the sociological analysis of roles, and is poor sociology. The value of analysing roles in terms of role sectors can be shown by considering an example already used, the role of the teacher, as composed of a number of role sectors, one for each of the sets of relationships, those with pupils, parents, fellow teachers, headmaster and school managers, that are involved in the role. Each of these groups may have rather different expectations of the teacher, and he may thus learn to vary his behaviour considerably according to which group he is in company with. But role sectors cannot neatly be compartmentalised, at least not by the people who are playing the roles. The teacher cannot altogether forget all the other groups to whom he must relate in his job when dealing with his pupils. Just as we cannot rigidly compartmentalise roles into role sectors, so it is also a mistake to see the various roles an individual plays as completely unrelated to each other. People do sometimes try to compartmentalise their lives, as did the Nazi concentration commandant who also saw himself as a kindly family man, or, more mildly perhaps, the intellectual socialist who enjoyed dining at expensive and exclusive restaurants. Others seem to have their lives compartmentalised for them, as in the case of the office tyrant who at home turns into the forlorn figure known as the 'henpecked' husband. But even in these cases, the way people play their roles is coloured by the other roles they perform. The individuality of role playing lies in that while any one role performance is liable to be influenced by the individual's other roles, the combination of roles possessed by any individual may be quite unique. To give very simple examples, the married teacher will be rather different from the single one, as will be the one who is a keen footballer from the one who is a spare-time musician. Further understanding of the relationship between the individual as a person and the various roles he plays requires us to consider the idea of the individual's self in relation to his roles.

ROLE AND SELF

When sociologists talk about the self, they are not usually referring to some deep inner personality, or the soul of the individual. Rather, self for the sociologist refers to the individual's conception of himself and the conception of himself that significant others hold. For the sociologist, the self is social, consisting of images of ourselves that are developed in the course of social action. At the outset, then, it should be clear that it is quite erroneous to think of the relation between role and self as a contrast between the roles of society and the individual role player's inner nature.

The concept of self utilised by sociologists in role analysis is dependent on the theories of members of the early Chicago school of American sociology, particularly those of C. H. Cooley and George Herbert Mead. Mead conceives of the self as composed of two components, the 'me' and the 'I'.[6] The 'me' constitutes our reflections of others' impressions of ourselves, which we obtain by placing ourselves in the role of these others. Thus, a mother's impression of herself as a mother will depend in part on her placing herself, in her imagination, in the role of her children, putting herself in their place in their relationship with her.

Often, the roles of others that we take are not those of specific individuals, but of generalised others. Thus, the mother takes the role of children in relation to mothers, and the magistrate, in developing his perception of himself as a magistrate, takes the roles of solicitors and policemen as generalised others, rather than the roles of the particular policeman and solicitors working in his court. As was pointed out in Chapter 3 (p. 66), the generalised others that are significant for the individual constitute his reference groups. There, it was seen that the individual defines his situation in terms of his reference groups; so also he may be seen to define himself in terms of his reference groups.

The process of role-taking may be seen, following Mead, to be fundamental in social communication. By taking the role of the other in social interaction, the individual assumes the attitudes of the other and is thus able to anticipate the response of the other to his own actions. To quote from Mead, in taking the role of the other, the individual

> . . . is in the role of the other person whom he is so exciting and influencing. It is through taking this role of the other that he is able to come back on himself and so direct his own process of communication. This taking the role of the other . . . is not simply of passing importance. It is not something that just happens as an incidental result of the gesture, but it is of importance in the development of co-operative activity. The immediate effect of such role-taking lies in the control which the individual is able to exercise over his own response.[7]

In taking the role of the other we assume the other's attitudes, and thereby seek to understand them, but this does not mean that we take them over as our own. The suspect takes the role of the policeman in his attempt to avoid the latter's questions, but he certainly does not take over the policeman's attitudes as his own. When we take over the attitudes of another as our own, we are taking the other's standpoint as well as his role.

The 'me' is the social component of self. If the self were seen solely as this component, it would be simply a passive product of the individual's reflection on others' impressions of him. The 'I' affirms that the individual's self is also very much a direct product of his own activity. The 'I' consists of the actual response of the individual to the attitudes of others: it is the creative element of self, spontaneous, uncertain, never fully predictable. No matter how carefully people plan their actions, they can never be quite sure – and less so their associates – that they will do exactly what they intended. Sometimes we 'get carried away with ourselves', as does the after-dinner speaker, well lubricated with wine, whose speech is rather longer and rather less discreet than he intended. On other occasions, we fluff our lines as when we are unable to articulate coherently, let alone plausibly, the perfect well-rehearsed excuse. The dread of many engaged in public speaking is that they might 'freeze', and be reduced to silence in their speeches. If sometimes we fail ourselves, it is also true that on occasion we excel ourselves: we manage to stand up to someone whom we thought would put us down easily, or we keep our tempers when we thought we would lose them. We can never be quite sure of our actions until we reflect on them afterwards, for it is only others in the situation who can experience our actions directly. Everyday notions such as getting carried away with ourselves, failing ourselves, excelling ourselves, or losing control of ourselves imply some split within the self, which can be rendered intelligible by conceiving the self as composed of the 'me' and the 'I'. The individual experiences his actions as part of the 'me', for he experiences them by reflecting upon them, and this reflection is influenced by his imagination of the impression of his actions on others. The 'I' of the past thus becomes the 'me' of the present. For Mead, the self is a process of interaction between the 'I' and the 'me'. It is these twin components of self, drawing the distinction between the active and the passive, the personal and the social, the spontaneous and the determined, that encapsulate the tensions and conflicts between the individual and society, not the distinction between role and self.

The notion of the self as dependent on reflections upon the impressions of others, utilised by Mead, was initially developed by Cooley with his notion of the 'looking-glass self'.[8] The individual sees himself, as it were, through the looking-glass of the reactions of others to him. Thus, to use very simple examples, one child regards himself as clever and good-looking, while another sees himself as dull and unattractive because these are the impressions that they perceive that others have of them. In forming his conception of himself, the individual imagines how he appears to others and how they judge that appearance. Here is the embryonic form of the 'me'. The 'I' is also implicit in Cooley's work, in that the conception of self is completed by the individual's reaction to others' perceived judgements of his appearance. The clever and good-looking boy may have feelings of pride, and the dull and unattractive one feelings of mortification. The self, then, is not something concrete, but is based on the individual's imagination of the impressions he makes on others in the process of social interaction and communication. As Mead puts it, in a discussion of Cooley's work,

The self is not an immediate character of the mind, but arises through the imagination of the ideas which others entertain of the individual, which has as its counterpart the organisation of our ideas of others into their selves. It is out of this bi-polar process that social individuals appear.[9]

The individual's conception of himself depends upon his imagination of other people's ideas about himself, but at the same time, in developing his ideas of himself, he attempts in his actions to control the impressions other people have of him. It may be that he tries to project an image of himself which he doesn't himself hold, in order to take advantage of the other party in the situation. Thus the salesman may attempt to project an image of himself as one who is genuinely concerned to serve the best interests of his customers; should the hapless customer be taken in, it will be easy to take advantage of him. Even if he projects an image of himself which he does hold, the individual may consciously control his actions to ensure that others will see this image correctly. The social worker who is genuinely concerned about her client may nevertheless find it necessary consciously to manipulate the image of herself she presents to the client lest he gains the wrong impression. Thus, she might feign an interest in certain activities of the client – perhaps his cinema-going, or stamp collecting – in order to maintain the genuinely held impression of herself as someone who is concerned with her client's problems.

In everyday language, we sometimes distinguish between a person's 'true' self, and the impression of himself that he tries to foster; between what someone is really like, and what he appears to be like. Yet this is only a distinction between different images of self, between the image a person has of himself and the images he sees that others have of him, or between the image we have of an individual and the image we see that he would like us to have of him. Thus, the student may see himself as really quite a lazy person though he is aware that he is regarded by others as exceptionally hard working, and the village do-gooder, impressing herself upon us as kind and altruistic, may seem to us to be really no more than a social climber. Just as the individual may take in others with a self-image that he does not believe in, so he may fail to persuade others to accept a self-image even though they perceive that he is himself taken in by it. So the politician may seek to convince his audience of his honour and integrity, but only manage to impress upon them that he has persuaded himself that he is of such character, despite all the evidence to the contrary. Furthermore, while a person may manipulate his projected self-image to gain advantages, as in the case of the apparently altruistic salesman, the individual may sometimes find that his own self-image has been manipulated by others so that they may gain advantage at his expense. Thus the student emphasises the importance of the research of his tutor in his essays in the hope of securing better grades, and the office junior laughs heartily at the feeble jokes of his boss in the hope of securing promotion.

The self is a product of social interaction, but at the same time may be manipulated by its owner and others to influence the course of social interaction, which in turn modifies the individual's conception of himself. As Goffman has put it:

> The self, then, as a performed character, is not an organic thing that has a specific location, whose fundamental fate is to be born, to mature and to die: it is a dramatic effect arising diffusely from a scene that is presented, and the characteristic issue, the crucial concern, is whether it will be discredited.[10]

As products of social interaction, the conceptions of himself that an individual holds and that others hold of him are derived from his performances in his social roles. According to Mead, for each role the individual plays there is a corresponding conception of self. The individual's total self-image is thus based on the summation of the selves of the individual in his various roles. Just as people do not compartmentalise their various selves, so performance in one role cannot be isolated from the other roles that the individual plays.

SPONTANEITY, INNOVATION AND IMPRESSION MANAGEMENT

The concept of role as defined in the first section of this chapter, in emphasising the societal perspective, provides a rather static and determinist view of roles. It is true that the individual may be seen as himself interpreting the expectations impinging upon him in his roles through his reference groups, but even so, the expectations are there for him to meet. Even though in some respects he may be allowed a measure of latitude or discretion, the basic role requirements would seem to be somewhat fixed and static. What is expected of him as a husband, father or teacher is defined by society, by the individual's reference groups, and seems to be independent of his own actions. But in real life, the roles people play are not fixed or static, but are continually modified in the course of social action, and are influenced by the actions of the role player himself. In the preceding discussion of the concept of self, it was shown how the passive, socially determined component of the self, the 'me', is counterbalanced with the active spontaneous component, the 'I'. Similarly, the determinist conception of role as set out for the individual by society needs to be counterbalanced by some conception which takes into account the spontaneous action of the individual in his role, and the processes which bring about changes in roles in the course of social interaction. The alternative is to be left with a form of role analysis which excludes human spontaneity and individuality.

A simple answer to the problem, and one that is often adopted by sociologists, is to distinguish role, as a set of expectations, from role performance, the actual behaviour of the individual in his role. Yet this may imply that while roles are social, role performances are individual and thereby beyond the sphere of the sociologist. The distinction may be useful in a limited sense for clarification, provided it is realised, as will be shown below, that roles are continually modified in the light of role performances.

A somewhat different approach, suggested by Ralph Turner, is to see roles as a process of role taking rather than as already laid out sets of expectations.[11] In the discussion of the concept of self (above, p. 80) it was seen how people learn the impressions others have formed of themselves by taking the roles of these others. Similarly, in role playing, the individual may be seen to take the role of the other, and then consider the other's conception of his own role before acting. Social interaction, seen as role playing, is thus based upon people's impressions of the roles of others, and their impressions of others' impressions of their own roles. Such impressions will be based upon knowledge of previous actions of the individuals involved, as well as upon social norms. Thus role definitions will be continually modified in the light of the responses, or role performances, with which they are confronted. As Ralph Turner has said,

> Interaction is always a *tentative* process, a process of continually testing the conception one has of the role of the other. The response of the other serves to reinforce or to challenge this conception. The product of the testing process is the stabilization or the modification of one's own role.[12]

To take the example of the classroom, the pupil is to be seen as continually modifying his conception of the teacher's role, and his ideas of the teacher's conception of his own role as pupil in the light of the events in the classroom. New teachers of boisterous classes often experience the process of being 'tested out' by their pupils, and should they succumb in these testing periods their future teaching experience with these classes may prove rather harrowing.

Now it may appear, from this example, that while the notion of role taking is useful for the study of interpersonal communication, it bears little relation to wider social influences – the influences of society on role playing. In role playing, people do not simply take the roles of the specific others in the situation, which is perhaps what the example emphasises, but they also take the roles of generalised others. Role taking is fundamental to the development of roles at any level, whether it be the role of one particular teacher or the role of teacher in general. Even generalised roles, corresponding to generalised others, are not fixed, but subject to modification in the course of social interaction. It was not very long ago, for example, that the role of the teacher in Britain was considered by teachers' employers, and teachers themselves, to be such as to rule out any possibility of strike action by teachers to improve salaries and conditions. Teachers' employers took this into account in their dealings with teachers, but more recently they have had to modify their view because teachers have gone on strike to improve their salaries and conditions. The imputed role of policeman may be modified by the individual citizen in the course of interaction with an individual policeman, but more general conceptions of the role of policemen may equally be modified following the wide-scale reporting of events involving policemen and demonstrators.

One very important implication of the notion of role taking is that the individual, by putting himself in the role of the other and assuming the other's attitude, may be able to work out the response required in order to evoke the appropriate attitude in the other, even though the individual does not himself share this attitude. In other words, in role playing, individuals learn how to manage and control the impressions they create in order to evoke the desired response in others. The pupil may learn the responses he must make to the teacher in order to conform to the teacher's conception of a 'good pupil', and he may well make these responses, not because he shares the values of the teacher, but in order to gain other more tangible benefits, such as a place in a school team which will mean missing lessons in order to travel to other schools. In this case, the pupil learns to convey an impression of himself to the teacher which is different from the impression he has of himself. It is the application of role analysis to the art of impression management that gives to role analysis the flavour of cynicism, epitomised in remarks such as those of Goffman that the sincere role player is one who is taken in by his own act. Such remarks are popularised in statements about politicians who supposedly devote such efforts to the portrayal of sincerity that eventually they come to believe themselves. But it is not necessarily cynical to view role playing in terms of impression management. If we were not able to control the impressions we make in order to mislead people as to our real intentions and our 'true' selves, then neither could we be sure that we would be able to impress upon people with any accuracy our real intentions and 'true' selves when we wished to be honest. Impression management is the basic technique whereby we control ourselves in social interaction, and as such it is fundamental to the process of meaningful social communication.

A brilliant analysis of the techniques people employ to control their impressions is given by Goffman in his *Presentation of Self in Everyday Life*, using an elaborated form of the dramatic analogy. A description of some of this analysis is worth while here. His style of presentation, which in its penetration and clarity is a sharp lesson to those academics who seem possessed of the curious belief that profundity is shown by dullness and obscurity, cannot be replicated.

In performing roles individuals attempt to convey a particular definition of the situation, and to persuade their audience to accept it, though they may or may not believe in it themselves. In this process, the role performer utilises various sorts of expressive equipment: he presents a 'front'. The 'front' consists of the setting for his role performance – the props, scenery and staging – and his personal front – his appearance and manner. The setting might be the businessman's office, with the mahogany desk, appropriate number of telephones, filing cabinets and other accoutrements to convey the desired impression of importance, status or hard work, or perhaps the living room of the businessman's home, designed to convey impressions of relaxation, cultural taste or mere opulence. Elements of the personal front are the clothes, the age, sex, looks, and manner of speech of the role player: all these elements are significant in the process of impression management, and all are consciously managed in role playing. For the social climber who affects the public school accent and manner, impression management is probably a more important part of his life, and probably a more time-consuming one than it is for most people, but even for those who do not wish to convey other than their 'natural' self, some attention must be paid to these matters lest they give the wrong impression.

Drawing on an analogy with the physical layout of the theatre, Goffman distinguishes between front regions where performances are given, and back regions, where they are prepared. As in the theatre, back regions are usually screened off from front regions, lest the audience of the performance should intrude behind the scenes. Thus, the hotel manager may be concerned to keep the door between the kitchens and the dining room closed, although the waitresses might prefer it to be kept open. Front and back regions should not be seen as fixed, but rather as situationally defined, and thus what may serve as a back region for one performance may well serve as a front region for another. For the teacher's classroom performance, the classroom is the front region, and the staff-room may serve as the back region where the performance is prepared. But in terms of interaction with other teachers, it is the staff-room that is the front region for the performance, and the teacher's home, or perhaps even his classroom, after the pupils have departed, that is the back region where the performance is prepared.

The notion of front and back regions implies that there are some situations where impressions must be managed very carefully, and others where we can relax, and perhaps just 'be ourselves'. It is certainly true that certain situations, such as those where we are being interviewed for a job, demand far more attention to impression management than others, but some attention to impression management is required in any interaction situation, even when we are 'just being ourselves' with close friends. Back regions may be seen as a series of receding regions, each more private than the preceding one. Perhaps the ultimate back region is the lavatory, for even if people on occasion share the bath, they would normally never share the lavatory closet.

Role performances are sometimes co-operative ventures, and thus Goffman uses the notion of 'team' to refer to a set of individuals co-operating in a single routine. Often, the impression fostered by the team before the audience cannot be maintained between members of the team, and thus teams are faced with the possibility that a member may give the show away by disclosing damaging information. Parents are faced with the problem that their children may reveal family secrets, as when a child naïvely reveals that his parents' excuse for not visiting a relative is not genuine. Political parties are faced with the problem that if internal disputes are not resolved, then a dissatisfied member, to further his cause, may reveal all to the newspapers.

Activity and revelation of information which is inconsistent with the definition of the situation which is being projected, which would tend to give the 'show' away, is described by Goffman as communication out of character. If teams have special problems in preventing the 'show' from being given away, even single role performers must guard against communication out of character, which would disrupt their performances. Performances sometimes tend to present idealised versions of the situation, and as such must conceal discrepancies between appearances and reality. Academics, in presenting idealised versions of their scholarship, sometimes learn techniques for concealing deficiencies in their learning from their students, so that they may make apparently perceptive comments on a book mentioned by a student of which in fact they know nothing. Acknowledged experts in various spheres may on occasion find it necessary to resort to improvisation and guesswork in order to maintain their image. Thus the political expert may give a seemingly authoritative explanation of an election result which he himself is aware is quite dubious.

There are many possibilities for communication out of character. The audience may suddenly appear while it is being ridiculed in its presumed absence, and to save the show, the performer will have to change the content of his communication in mid-sentence without a telltale pause. The suppression of communication out of character may require considerable self-control, for performances may be disrupted by discordant expressions of anger or mirth. Team members, though, may be able to convey out-of-character communication to each other during performances, while concealing this communication from the audience. Human perception is such that it is relatively easy, for example, for us to catch the eye of one individual without revealing this to others who may be present. Communication may also be such that in a single item of communication the performer may convey one meaning to his audience, and an additional, quite different one, to a fellow team member who shares some of his secrets. Thus a married couple, on being invited to view their neighbour's efforts at interior decoration, may be able to impress upon the neighbour how much they like it while at the same time indicating to each other how much they dislike it. Should the couple, however, become too bold in their game to outdo each other in their false praises, there is a danger that a discrepant smile, or perhaps a complete breakdown of social control shown in sudden peals of inadequately suppressed laughter, may give the show away. If this happens, then acute embarrassment all round is likely to be the consequence.

Generally, it may be said that when the definition of the situation presented by the role performer is no longer credible for the audience, embarrassment is the probable consequence, embarrassment for both the performer and the audience. It is for this reason that audiences tend to ignore inconsistencies in role performances and to accept as long as they can the projected definition of the situation. Even where the inconsistencies are such that the projected definition of the situation is no longer credible, audiences may still be tactful and pretend to accept the projected definition. Thus, even if the man who is showing his neighbours his new interior decoration becomes aware that their praises are feigned, he is unlikely to seek to expose the reality behind the façade. Whether a role performance is true or false from the point of view of the audience, however, usually depends not upon the competence of the performance, but on whether or not the performer is authorised to play the role. An individual may perform the role of clergyman quite competently and plausibly, but his performance will be judged fraudulent if it is discovered that he is not, in fact, entitled to perform this role. Goffman notes that the competent performance of roles by impostors may cast doubts upon the skills claimed by the legitimate role performers.

The fundamental concern of Goffman's study is the analysis of techniques whereby role performers maintain their projected definition of the situation, and how they cope with the many factors which continually threaten to disrupt it.

This report . . . is concerned with the structure of social encounters – the structure of those entities in social life that come into being whenever persons enter one another's immediate physical presence. The key factor in this structure is the maintenance of a single definition of the situation, this definition having to be expressed, and this expression sustained in the face of a multitude of potential disruptions.[13]

For some sociologists, such as Alvin Gouldner,[14] the significance of Goffman's work would appear to lie in the presumed implication that social life is a mere façade, a world of appearances. It is certainly the case that Goffman does lend some credence to a rather cynical view of social life, as has been already noted (p. 87). In discussing the relationship between appearances and reality, Goffman suggests that from the point of view of the performance, what is important is not whether the performer is sincere or insincere, but whether or not he *appears* to be sincere: furthermore, the appearance of sincerity may be best conveyed not by complete honesty, but by skilful blending of sincerity and contrivance.

> a rigid incapacity to depart from one's inward view of reality may at times endanger one's performance. Some performances are carried off successfully with complete dishonesty, others with complete honesty; but for performances in general, neither of these extremes is essential, and neither, perhaps, is dramaturgically advisable.[15]

However, the real significance of Goffman's work, which is the reason for its extended treatment here, lies in his presentation of role playing not as the mechanistic performance of predetermined roles laid out by society, but as a creative, imaginative, and essentially human activity. By viewing role playing as impression management, we see how the individual develops his roles in his imagination, and, in projecting the image that he has developed, creates and modifies his roles in his performance.

Probably no sociologist really sees social interaction as mechanistic and predetermined. Those who do employ a somewhat determinist conception excuse themselves, as Dahrendorf does, with the following disclaimer:

> However we turn and twist *homo sociologicus*, he will never be the particular person who is our friend, colleague, father or brother. *Homo sociologicus* can neither love, nor hate, laugh nor cry. He remains a pale, incomplete, strange, artificial man.[16]

And so Dahrendorf introduces the notion of the 'private character' of man, which is beyond sociological investigation. Yet in Goffman's work, individual spontaneity is taken into account in the analysis of the structure of social encounters. This is most notably so in his treatment of role distance, which is discussed later in this chapter. We do not need to construct a mystical 'private character' of man if we avoid a dehumanised sociology.

ROLE CONFLICT AND ROLE DISTANCE

Primarily from the standpoint of the perspective of society, role has been defined as a set of expectations. From this, the discussion proceeded to consider the relation between role and self, and here it emerged that the tension between social determination and individual spontaneity was represented not by the contrast between role and self, but by the tension between the two components of self, the 'me' and the 'I'. If both components are to be found in self, then both should be found in role as well. Hence the discussion proceeded to focus on individualistic aspects of role, considering the process of role taking and the technique of impression management in role playing. In noting that any individual plays a number of roles, some brief consideration has been given to the extent to which these can be seen as compartmentalised, but there has yet been no systematic consideration of the relations between the different roles that any one individual plays. This is the task now to be addressed, and here again, the tension between social determinism and individual spontaneity, throwing into contrast the societal and individualistic perspectives, will emerge as significant.

The individual in society, playing his various social roles, is subject to a set of expectations for each of them: taking all his roles together, it is more than likely that not all the expectations he will be faced with will be quite compatible, and some may even be in direct conflict. Role conflict describes the situation in which the individual is faced with such incompatible or conflicting expectations in his various roles, and it is a situation with which, in one form or another, most people must learn to cope. Most obvious, perhaps, are the conflicts between the familial, occupational and leisure roles. Certain occupations may make demands, such as evening work, or being away from home for long periods, which may be incompatible with the demands of family life. The athletic student may find the training and other demands of his sporting roles incompatible with the demands of his studies. Sometimes, as may be the case in the above examples, it may not be that the expectations of the different roles are directly in conflict, but rather that the individual does not possess the resources of time and energy to fulfil all of them adequately. Common sense might suggest that the more roles an individual plays the more difficult it becomes for him to meet the expectations of all of them, but the evidence of sociological research shows that this is not necessarily the case. Research on activity in voluntary associations has indicated that the more organisations an individual belongs to, then the more likely he is to be active in all of them.[17] The author, in interviewing members of political parties in Liverpool, found that people with quite vast ranges of voluntary activities – one man was a member of no less than seventeen committees – very easily made themselves available for interview, whereas those who were always too busy to be seen appeared, if and when they were finally interviewed, to have relatively little with which to occupy their time. Direct role conflict is likely to occur when, in an encounter, an individual confronts another in two or more roles simultaneously. Suppose, at auditions for a play, the theatrical director finds one of these taking part to be a close relative. In deciding whether to award a part to this relative, should he act solely in his role as director, or in his role, say, as father-in-law? The former role would demand that purely theatrical considerations should determine the decision, whereas the latter would involve the consideration of other, personal factors. Such role conflict, the simultaneous playing of more than one role in one situation, is legally recognised in Britain. Thus, in local government, councillors are required to declare any pecuniary interest they may have in matters under consideration in council, and having made such a declaration, they are not allowed to vote on the matter except by special dispensation. Failure to declare interests may incur severe legal penalties. There are, for example, what are known as 'conflicts of interests' for a councillor who is a property owner if the council is considering an application for planning permission on the particular property that he owns, or for the councillor who is a council-house tenant when the council reviews council-house rents. These are examples of direct role conflict.

So far, the discussion has been concerned with conflicts between the different roles an individual plays. Role conflict may also occur within a single role. Earlier in this chapter (p. 77) it was suggested that roles might be seen as sets of role sectors, and from this formulation it may be seen that expectations deriving from the different sectors of a single role may be in conflict. Classic instances of this are the role of foreman, involving conflicting expectations from shop-floor workers and management, and the role of non-commissioned officer in the Army, involving conflicting expectations from officers and other ranks. Management expects the foreman to be loyal to their objectives, whereas the men on the shop-floor may expect a different sort of loyalty from someone whom they believe ought to be 'one of the lads', and the situation may be somewhat similar for the non-commissioned officer. The larger the number of different groups of people to which the individual has to relate in playing his role, the greater are the possibilities for the expectations impinging from the different sectors to come into conflict. Some research has suggested that role strain and role conflicts are more likely to occur in roles which are composed of a large number of sectors than in those involving more limited social interaction.[18] Thus, one American study[19] found the occupation of waitress to be somewhat stressful, and that it was not unusual for waitresses to burst into tears. This could be explained in terms of the variety of different sorts of people with whom the waitress was required to communicate in the course of her work. These would include her supervisors, service pantry workers, cooks, other waitresses and waiters, as well as her customers, and thus at times, when both the kitchen and customers are becoming irate, the waitress may feel unable to cope.

How do people cope with role conflict? Faced with role conflicts the individual cannot merely fulfil society's expectations in his roles, because the fulfilling of some of the requirements entails the neglect of others: he must make a choice. Role conflict thus points to one aspect of the assertion of the individual against the social determination of role, though the choice made by the individual in a situation of role conflict is itself subject to social influences. Various techniques whereby people may resolve role conflicts and decide on appropriate courses of action in the face of incompatible expectations have been described by sociologists.[20] He may, for example, attempt to compartmentalise his roles, or the sectors of a particular role. Thus, the businessman who finds the demands of the business world and family life incompatible may attempt to ensure that his business and family life are kept separate, and may be somewhat disconcerted should his wife suddenly appear in his office, or his secretary at his home. The professor may be able to cope with the incompatible demands of his vice-chancellor and his teaching staff so long as he never has to face both simultaneously. Alternatively, the individual may decide to neglect the expectations of those who are least powerful in the situation, which will minimise the possibility of unpleasant repercussions. The college teacher who is summoned to a committee meeting by the principal at the same time that he is supposed to be teaching might, therefore, following this rationale, choose to neglect his students. Sometimes the individual may be faced with a choice between meeting certain expectations which he feels he ought to meet, and fulfilling other expectations which carry substantial rewards or penalties. Thus, the police chief might have to decide between his career prospects, together with the fortunes of his force, and the prosecution of a group of influential politicians for corruption.

In the above discussion, role conflict appears to result in the individual making fairly clear 'either–or' choices between alternative role expectations. Such clear-cut cases do occur. Should a doctor tell the parents of the confessions of one of his teenage patients? Should he put confidentiality, or, as he sees it, the welfare of his patient first? A recent case of this nature attracted considerable public attention. Yet it is mistaken to see all role conflict in this way, a mistake deriving from a view of role expectations as somewhat fixed, which we must either conform to or deviate from. If role is seen as a process, continually modified in the course of social interaction, role performance becomes a process of adapting oneself to one's role and one's role to oneself, rather than a simple issue of conformity or deviance.[21] Adaptation to role conflict is perhaps often more like the steering of a tortuous route to avoid obstacles and pitfalls, using the various techniques of impression management, rather than a choice between two clearly marked paths.

While it has been suggested (p. 82) that the tension between the individual and society is not reflected in the relationship between role and self, in everyday life, people do sometimes make a quite conscious divorce between role and self, so that conflict between role and self may appear to be one form of role conflict. As will be seen, such apparent conflicts in reality represent techniques employed by people to cope with role conflict, rather than inherent conflicts in themselves. When people perform distasteful roles, or aspects of otherwise agreeable roles that are distasteful, they sometimes claim that they are only doing what they have to, and they therefore imply that their true character is not to be judged by their current activities. In this way, people may attempt to diminish their responsibility for their actions. Such pleas are characteristic defences of those tried for war crimes, who claim that they were only obeying orders. At a rather different level, the bailiff who proceeds to evict a family from their home and leave them forlorn, together with their furniture and belongings, in the street outside, may express sympathy for the family's hardship, but at the same time point out that he is only doing what he has to do in his job. Peter Berger[22] has argued that one of the lessons of sociology is that people do not have to do what is set out for them in their roles, but are free to choose whether they will follow the dictates of their roles or their consciences. The individual who follows a course of action which he believes to be morally wrong because he sees he has no choice in the role laid out for him, is therefore acting in bad faith. He is opting out of his moral responsibility by proclaiming himself to be socially determined in his situation and thereby unable to make choices. The mechanistic conception of sociological man as a socially determined role player becomes a device whereby the individual may abrogate all moral responsibility for his actions. This is no obscure point of social theory, but one of crucial significance in the world today. There is no doubt that soldiers, politicians, bureaucrats and industrialists, people whose actions have profound effects upon the lives of others, do disclaim moral responsibility for their actions in this way, and that a mechanistic sociology can be used to justify their actions. However, as Berger argues, a humanistic sociology can do much to counteract such reasoning, and advance the realisation of human freedom by showing how it is possible to escape from the constraints of the image of social determinism.

Apparent conflicts between role and self may be analysed socio-logically through means of the concept of role distance, which has been developed by Erving Goffman. That such conflicts are always apparent rather than real will emerge from the subsequent discussion. Role distance refers to the impression given by the individual that he is not fully involved in or contained by the definition of the situation portrayed in his role performance. He makes communications out of character with the role in order to show that he is something more than the role he is playing in the situation. He is thus attempting to indicate some discrepancy between role and self. So the traffic warden who compliments the flowers bought by an erring lady motorist, the shop assistant who advises her customer that a better bargain may be obtained elsewhere, the lecturer who digresses into personal anecdotes, the clergyman who tells biblical jokes at churchly gatherings, parents who proclaim to each other that they have only embarked on the seaside boat trip for the sake of their children, even the celebrated young man, who, in varying social situations, says: 'I'm only here for the beer', all are taking distance from their role in the situation. They are all saying 'I'm not just someone who does this particular job, you know', or perhaps even 'I'm not really the sort of person that you would expect to find doing this sort of thing'. It is not that people taking role distance are necessarily unwilling performers of their roles, but rather that they are concerned to show that they are 'real people', perhaps, something more than the particular roles that they happen to be playing. The traffic warden may have every confidence in the value of his work, but aware of derogatory stereotypes built up of him among the motoring public may be concerned to show that he is more than just a traffic warden. Sometimes, indeed, role distance may be displayed to conceal involvement in role performance that might be considered inappropriate. Thus, the man buying a train set for his son might deliberately affect role distance to conceal his engrossment in playing with the train himself.

Goffman uses the merry-go-round to illustrate the notion of role distance by describing the actions of different age groups when riding on the merry-go-round. Before the age of three or four, children may be unable to cope with the role of merry-go-round rider. They may become frantic, so that the machine will have to be stopped so they can be taken off. Three- or four-year-old children can just about cope with the role demands, and they take the merry-go-round very seriously, and are very much involved in the role. After this age, however, children begin to take distance from the role of merry-go-round rider. The five-year-old

> may keep time to the music by clapping his feet or a hand against the horse, an early sign of utter control. Another may make a wary stab at standing on the saddle or changing horses without touching the platform. Irreverence begins, and the horse may be held by his wooden ear or his tail. The child says by his actions: 'Whatever I am, I'm not just someone who can barely manage to stay on a wooden horse'.

At seven or eight:

> . . . the child not only dissociates himself self-consciously from the kind of horseman a merry-go-round allows him to be but also finds many of the devices that younger people use for this are now beneath him. He rides no-hands, gleefully chooses a tiger or a frog as a steed, clasps hands with a mounted friend across the aisle.

At eleven or twelve,

> . . . maleness for boys has become a real responsibility, and no easy means of role distance seems to be available on merry-go-rounds.

It is necessary to stay away or to exert creative acts of distance, as
when a boy jokingly treats his wooden horse as though it were a
racing one.

There are adult techniques for coping with the merry-go-round[23] too,
demonstrated by the young couple who go on it for a laugh, and the
parent sitting next to his two-and-a-half-year-old, who indicates, as
does the man who runs the machine, that for him the ride is not an
event. Goffman's example is both ingenious and intriguing.

Goffman distinguishes a number of dimensions of role involvement,
which serve for clarification in the analysis of role distance. Individuals
may or may not be *committed* to the roles they play, which is a matter
of structural arrangements and not of the performance. People are
normally committed to their occupational roles, because their income
depends on these roles. The role of parent, too, usually involves
commitment, for parents are generally required to look after and
provide for their children. People become *attached* to roles when they
identify themselves with the roles they play. Some people may do the
football pools each week in the faint hope that they may escape from
occupational roles to which they are committed but not attached. On
the other hand, other people, such as amateur actors, may be strongly
attached to roles to which they are hardly committed. Attachment to
a role may or may not be revealed in its performance, and the taking
of role distance indicates a certain lack of attachment, even though, in
the case of the sportsman putting on a brave face in defeat, the lack
of attachment may be feigned. *Embracement* is a characteristic not of
the individual's attitude to his role, but of its actual performance.
Individuals embrace roles when they appear to be attached to them,
show all the capacities required, and are totally involved in the role
performance.

> To embrace a role is to disappear completely into the virtual self
> available in the situation, to be seen fully in terms of the image, and
> to confirm expressively one's acceptance of it.[24]

As one example, Goffman gives the policeman on point duty at a very
busy road junction, whose every bodily movement is a part of the
role he plays. Other examples might be the grandmaster chess player,
or the championship golfer at the last putt. Both may complain about
background incidents which may work against total embracement of

the role. The chess player may be disturbed by the noise of film cameras and coughs from the audience, and the golfer may be disturbed by the clicking of camera shutters, or even worse, the noise of transistor radios.

Total role embracement represents the polar opposite of role distance. Embracement may be feigned to conceal a lack of attachment to the role, as in the case of the academic who takes pains to appear serious and scholarly lest he reveal that he has lost interest in his subject. Similarly, as has been noted, role distance may be feigned to conceal an attachment to a role which might not appear seemly. Furthermore, both role embracement and role distance may be manipulated for dramatic effect in the performance of a role. If the performance of the role requires great skill, then the display of role distance in the course of the performance may serve to emphasise the skill of the performer. The business executive at a conference who makes penetrating and perceptive remarks about the discussion on hand doubly impresses his audience if he has apparently been asleep during most of the proceedings. On the other hand, a display of role embracement may serve to impress upon the audience the great skill and concentration that is required to perform the role. Thus the circus flying trapeze act is preceded by a request from the ringmaster for silence from the audience, followed by a roll of drums. Sometimes, the artists are very much engaged audibly and visibly to the audience in communication over the timing of the act. This may well be necessary, because often such acts are highly dangerous for the performers, but the point is that there is no need to conceal it because it heightens rather than reduces the dramatic effect of the performance.

Role distance is thus a device whereby the individual may show spontaneity, creativity and imagination in the role he plays, whereby he may show that he is something more than the role player in the situation. It is a device whereby he may show that his self is not truly reflected in the role he happens to play. Yet, as was shown above (p. 84), the images people have of themselves are derived from and correspond to the roles that they play. Role distance is in reality not so much the assertion of the self as something independent of the individual role, but rather the penetration of the individual's various other roles into his ongoing role performance. Just as people do not compartmentalise their various selves, so performance in one role cannot be isolated from all the other roles that the individual plays.

... the individual does not embrace the situated role that he finds available to him whilst holding all his other selves in abeyance ... a situated activity system provides an arena for conduct and ... in this arena the individual constantly twists, turns and squirms, even while allowing himself to be carried along by the controlling definition of the situation. The image that emerges of the individual is that of a juggler and synthesiser, an accomodator and appeaser, who fulfils one function while he is apparently engaged in another; he stands guard at the door of the tent but lets all his friends and relatives crawl in under the flap.[25]

Role distance, then, describes the process whereby the elements of the individual's self derived from other roles creep into the current situation and affect the performance of the given role in the situation. It may serve as a device for coping with role conflict, a device whereby a person shows that he is not attached to a particular role which is inconsistent with other roles that he plays. Thus, role distance for the twelve-year-old merry-go-round rider indicates that he is not attached to a role which is inconsistent with his age role. However, I hope the discussion of role distance has shown that its significance goes far beyond the issue of role conflict. It is because people are not rigidly compartmentalised into the roles they play that role distance is, as Goffman points out, not something unusual, but is in fact typical of role performance in everyday life. Role distance points to the individuality of the person in the role he plays, but individuality that derives from the social contexts of the other roles that he plays.

THE DRAMATIC ANALOGY

It is the dramatic analogy from which the concept of role in sociology is derived: people play roles in the real world – as workers, teachers, parents, club members, and so on – just as actors play roles on the stage. The basic analogy as employed by sociologists reflects the words of Shakespeare in *As You Like It*, oft quoted, but unsurpassable.

> All the world's a stage,
> And all the men and women merely players:
> They have their exits and their entrances;
> And one man in his time plays many parts,
> His act being seven ages.

Shakespeare goes on to describe the various age roles of man. But in fact, while the analogy highlights several aspects of the role concept, sociologists depart from it on a number of crucial points. Some reflection on the dramatic analogy will thus serve as a useful conclusion to this chapter.

The first thing to be noticed about the dramatic analogy is the image it provides of social determinism in role playing. Stage actors follow prepared scripts, and thus, by analogy, role players in the real world get their scripts, their expectations, from society. Yet it is in the work of Goffman that the dramatic analogy is developed in its most elaborate form, utilising a host of theatrically derived concepts such as props, scenery, staging, front and back regions, even describing role performance as a show: and it is Goffman, I have suggested, who presents a particularly human and creative conception of role. In Goffman's work, it is not society that provides the script so much as the role players themselves who improvise their own. The script is not, however, the performance, but only the plan of the performance, and even if we have produced it ourselves, we can still fluff our lines. To return to the concept of self here, the script corresponds to the 'me' and the performance to the 'I'.

The second issue raised by the dramatic analogy is more philosophical than sociological. It is the complaint that the social world, viewed as actors playing parts for dramatic effect, may be made to appear as shallow and artificial, a world of empty façades, tricks and illusions. Thus Alvin Gouldner has criticised Goffman for presenting a social world purely of appearances, a world in which what counts is not what a man does, but what he appears to do.

> Goffman thus declares a moratorium on the conventional distinction between make-believe and reality, or between the cynical and sincere. In this all-the-world's a stage world, what is taken to be real is not the work men do or the social functions they perform. . . . A man's value in this world . . . depends upon his appearance and not . . . on his talents, abilities, or achievements.[26]

Gouldner is concerned about the social influence of a sociology which puts such emphasis on appearances. Now it could, alternatively, be argued that the characterisation of social life as the manipulation of appearances is an accurate representation of social life today, especially in highly urbanised and industrialised environments, that social life is in fact shallow and superficial. The complaint then becomes one of general social criticism, rather than the criticism of sociology. In a very general sense, it is sometimes argued that the very notion of role playing implies an alienated form of social life, an alienation of the individual's conscious activities from his true self and human nature. Following this argument, it may be said that in playing a role, the individual lives at a stage removed from an awareness of his relationship with his environment: his consciousness is divorced from human nature. This may seem somewhat obscure, but perhaps may be illustrated by the tourist who, surrounded by beautiful scenery, is concerned to say appropriate things to his companion in order to impress upon him his sensitivity to nature, or to take photographs to impress his friends rather than to enjoy the experience. At Corrieshalloch Gorge, a well-known beauty spot in Wester Ross, Scotland, the best view can be obtained from a small platform, which is capable of carrying only two people at a time. In the summer season, queues may develop to stand on this platform. Recently, waiting in such a queue, I observed that several tourists in their brief pause on the platform never removed their eyes from the viewfinders of their cameras.

In social life, we have perhaps all experienced relationships with those who are always so concerned with the impressions that they are making upon us that they never seem to express any true feelings. One could, of course, be cynical and suggest that such people are just those who are not very good at conveying the impression of sincerity! Role playing may involve shallowness and superficiality, but this is not necessarily the case. It is a mistake to think that the characterisation of social life as role playing on the basis of the dramatic analogy involves such a view of man, a mistake deriving from a misuse of the analogy.

Care must be taken in employing analogies in sociology, because argument by analogy tends to be based upon superficial similarities, rather than logical structuring, and to build complex theories solely on the basis of analogy would be a very dubious exercise. A basic mistake which can be made as a result of the dramatic analogy is to suggest that role playing in everyday life is like acting in the theatre, and with this mistake we have conceptions of society and social life as drama, comedy, farce or tragedy as is appropriate. But everyday life is *not* like the theatre. In using the dramatic analogy, Goffman makes it clear that he is *not* concerned with aspects of the theatre that creep into everyday life.[27] The dramatic analogy is only a framework, a scaffolding, for the analysis of the structuring of everyday life, but a framework that goes much beyond the basic analogy.

To begin with, roles are not put on and cast off in everyday life as they are in the theatre. The images we have of ourselves, our experrience of ourselves, derive from the roles we play: in a real sense, we are the roles we play. As Robert E. Park once put it:

Everyone is always and everywhere, more or less consciously, playing a role. . . . It is in these roles that we know each other; it is in these roles that we know ourselves.[28]

The best way, however, to show how the role framework goes beyond the simple dramatic analogy is to use it to analyse the world of the theatre itself. In order to do this, we must, as Goffman does,[29] distinguish between *playing* a role and *playing at* a role. A role that is played at is a make-believe role, and the audience is not expected to believe that the actor *is* the role he plays at. A stage actor playing *at* the role of jealous husband is playing the role of actor, and it is the role of actor which is real, which he takes seriously, and in the role of actor which he expects his audience to judge him. It is because the actor plays to an audience beyond the action and not to his fellow make-believe play actors that acting on the stage is quite different from everyday life role playing. In everyday life, extreme displays of emotion may be distressing, embarrassing or offensive, but in the theatre they may grip the audience and bring much applause at the curtain call. Actors on stage are expected to display what in everyday life we are expected to conceal. At the same time, the role of actor requires that its player appear credible as a real person in the make-believe role he is playing at. It is perhaps paradoxical that it is the very attempt of the stage actor to convey the impression of a real life scene to his audience that makes the scene so different from real life; for this is his purpose, and the only impression that counts to his fellow actors on the stage scene is that of his competence as an actor. Indeed, in order to impress his skill upon his fellow actors, the actor may take distance from his role and thus show them that he is not engrossed in his part in the way he appears to be to the audience. I once heard the story of a famous actor, who, with his back to the audience, gripped them with a display of grief, while at the same time he was managing to communicate to someone backstage his preferred horse in the next race. Total embracement in the make-believe role he is playing at is not usually* the mark of a good actor, and may indicate to his

* Though in the case of Method acting, it is.

colleagues that he is living the part he is cast in rather than the role of actor in the part, and is thus merely type cast.

It should not be thought that because the stage scene in the theatre differs from real life that playing at roles is not a part of everyday life. Apart from professional and amateur actors, and the make-believe of children, playing at roles occurs very commonly as a form of humour: the office junior plays at the boss and thus makes peremptory demands upon his secretary, who may return play with an excessive display of deference and servility. The schoolboy playing at teacher, and the soldier at sergeant-major, both about to be discovered by those they lampoon, are themes that have been used by cartoonists. Humour is perhaps an essential ingredient of everyday life, and it may well be useful for the sociologist to study the significance of playing at roles in everyday life. The point of introducing the notion here has been to distinguish it from role playing, and thereby show how the idea of role playing in sociology departs from and goes beyond the dramatic analogy.

5. Negatives in Social Organisation: Alienation and Deviance

This chapter is concerned with those apparently negative aspects of social life, the occasions where people do not adhere to the expected social norms, where they do not identify with the roles they play, but are alienated from them. The concepts of deviance and alienation provide a sociological framework for analysing such activity. The concern here is with what is sometimes called social pathology, but this is a somewhat dubious term, suggesting that problems of deviance, alienation and conflict in society are like some sort of social disease, and were they to be eliminated, society would be a perfectly functioning system. The idea of a perfectly functioning social system, in which everyone harmoniously fits into the roles laid out for them, in which conflicts and disagreements and all forms of deviance are somehow eliminated, would seem to imply the most rigid sort of social determinism and the denial of human freedom, and indeed of humanity itself. It also gives the impression that the social system will through its own workings manage any social problems that arise, that therefore social action to cope with these is unnecessary, and if we think things away they will go away anyway. It is best, therefore, to forget about such ideals as perfectly functioning systems, and to discard ideas of social disease and social pathology as well.

Deviance and alienation are sometimes regarded as more or less synonymous. Thus, it may be said that the deviant, in the classic form of the teenage vandal, is alienated from society, in that he fails to identify with society and accept his responsibilities as a member of it. What this really means is that he is alienated because he is not adjusted to society: adjusted people presumably conform. Used in this way, the notion of alienation is not very informative, except perhaps to suggest, in a pseudo-social-scientific fashion, that the deviant is rather nasty and anti-social. Thus, we are told, the political deviant, in the form of the left-wing 'fellow traveller', is alienated and possessed of various other unsavoury character traits as well.[1] More will be said below about this sort of usage of the concept of alienation: here the point is merely to note the popular association between alienation and deviance. It will be shown in this chapter that the relationship between the concepts is very complex, and that far from being synonymous, they may represent radically different sociological approaches. In fact, it is sometimes the conformist rather than the deviant who is most appropriately described as an alienated individual.

ALIENATION AND SOCIAL ROLES

The essential sociological significance of the concept of alienation cannot be made clearer than by placing it in the context of role playing. To put things in their simplest form we could say that the individual who does not identify with the role he plays is alienated from it, but, as will be seen shortly, such a simple formulation may conceal very contradictory applications of the term alienation. If we take the role of citizen, it may be said that this role in Western societies entails some minimal participation in politics by voting in elections. Thus, the non-voter is sometimes regarded as alienated – alienated from his citizen role of voter. This may be because the alienated citizen thinks that his vote will not influence the outcome of political events, or perhaps because he thinks that there is no real choice: all the political parties seem very much the same and led by the same sort of people. From whatever point of view this situation is approached, political alienation as we have described it represents at the very least a negative feature of political life in society. Yet the problem may be seen in very different ways. Frequently the problem is seen as one of the ability of the political system to cope with political alienation. If too many people are alienated and refrain from voting, then the validity and legitimacy of the election results begins to be questioned by more and more people, and so the 'democratic' political system is threatened. As A. W. Finifter has put it, 'alienation is commonly regarded as a threat to the survival of the political system'.[2] The problem is the problem of the system having to cope with alienated individuals, not that of individuals having to cope with an alienating system. As Robert E. Lane suggests, the alienated in politics are those who feel discontented with politics, whereas the non-alienated are those who are happy with the political system 'pretty much the way things are now'.[3] The political system only requires to be modified to ensure that enough people are sufficiently motivated to do what is required to maintain it, that enough people are happy with things 'pretty much the way things are now'. Lane, writing about the American political system in 1966, thinks that most people are happy with the way things are. If this approach to alienation is looked at in the language of role analysis, it would seem that alienation only occurs when people do not meekly accept the roles prepared for them but ask awkward questions and make awkward demands – perhaps asking whether the political system confers on them the benefits it is supposed to and demanding that perhaps they might have a voice in things. The opposite of alienation in this sense is not freedom, but adjustment. It is in this usage that alienation becomes synonymous with deviance: the politically alienated, discontented and distrusting people are also politically deviant. People who do not accept things as they are, then, are to be regarded as alienated, and so alienation in the sense discussed is revealed as an ideological concept of conservative thought. This is not in itself a condemnation, for most sociological concepts have ideological connotations. The real objection is that such a usage denudes of serious meaning a concept which has profound implications for sociology. It also directly contradicts the treatment of alienation in the Marxian tradition, even though those sociologists employing it take Marx as their basic starting point. In this tradition, the society in which everyone willingly adjusts to the roles of the political system, in which everyone serves the system's requirements, is a society characterised by alienation rather than the absence of alienation. This is because the exercise of political power becomes divorced from the decision-making of individuals and rests in the impersonal operations of an objectified system. Social and political systems are in reality relationships between people, produced by the activities of people. Alienation is present when such systems confront people as external forces over which they have no control. The non-voter is alienated, not because he is discontented with the political system but because the political system confronts him as an external, alien force over which he has no control, and in which he has no part. It may be helpful here to provide a more concrete example of political alienation. At a meeting of a local Labour Party at which the author was present, a long-standing member, who had held several offices in the local party, was complaining about the way she, and people like her, had been treated by the party. She had worked for the party for years, but the party had done nothing for her or for her district: the party had not even provided a social club for its members. The party was seen as some impersonal force, standing over and above the individual member. Yet the party as an organisation is nothing more than the social relationships between its members. For the member in question, these relationships are transposed into some alien objective entity – the party – though it is still the product of herself and people like her. In this example, I have attempted to parallel Karl Marx's depiction of the alienation of labour:

> . . . the object which labor produces – labor's product – confronts it as *something alien*, as a *power independent* of the producer.
> . . . the worker is related to the *product of his labor* as to an *alien* object.
> . . . the more the worker spends himself, the more powerful becomes the alien world of objects which he creates over and against himself, the poorer he himself – his inner world – becomes, the less belongs to him as his own.[4]

Marx develops this argument from the conditions of capitalism, in which labour is exploited and enslaved by capital, which is itself the product of labour. For Marx, in his *Economic and Philosophic Manuscripts* of 1844, alienation comprises three elements, namely the alienation of the worker from the product of his labour, the alienation of his productive activity, so that his own activity becomes an alien activity and as such alienates the worker from himself, and finally, the alienation of man from his 'species being'.[5] The last named element is particularly obscure and requires some explanation.

According to Marx, man is distinguished from animals in that he alone engages in free, conscious, productive life-activity.[6] Animals produce only to serve their immediate needs, whereas man can choose to produce and create over and above his needs. Conscious, productive life activity is therefore the species character of man, and man is alienated from his species being when this life activity is not recognised as such, but instead becomes only a means to existence. Life itself is devalued when it becomes only a means to life. Man's life is his activity, and if this activity is alien to him – working instrumentally in return for a wage, and watching the clock all the time – then it can be said that man is alienated from himself. The alienation of man from himself – self-estrangement – and the alienation of man from his species being are thus closely linked. Both are philosophical notions, based on values concerning the nature of man, his activities and his relationship to nature, but they are of considerable sociological importance. Alienation is inevitably a value concept, because it implies alienation from something – some ideal standard. As we have seen, with alienation defined as the opposite to adjustment, the ideal standard becomes the *status quo*. Because alienation is a value concept there are difficulties in relating it to other sociological concepts, as will be seen below.

Marx's focus in his discussion of alienation is the alienation of labour. Thus, alienation is frequently seen as a problem of the contemporary work situation, particularly in occupations involving routine and monotonous work. Yet it is quite wrong to think that Marx equated labour merely with work in the sense of paid employment. Labour for Marx is creative and productive life activity, productive in the sense of enhancing and developing man, not in the sense of production of commodities valued in money terms. Today, productive work is often taken to be synonymous with commodity production: even the amateur decorator and amateur gardener may assess their efforts in terms of how much it would have cost to pay someone to do the decorating, or how much it would cost to buy the garden produce. In Marxian terms, this represents alienation. The intrinsic value of labour is replaced by its exchange value in monetary terms, and labour itself becomes a commodity, valued simply as a means of exchange. Erich Fromm has suggested that modern society is characterised by the tendency for all activities to be valued only in exchange terms, and as such to be reduced to abstract monetary values.[7] Thus, the concertgoer considers whether his seat is 'worth the money', and the value of a course of education is assessed in terms of monetary value – the extra income the student will be able to earn, or his contribution to the 'economy', in relation to the cost of education. In the planning of urban motorways, it is considered to be humanitarian to assess social costs – the disruption of family and community life – as well as the direct costs of land acquisition and construction. Yet this involves the reduction of family and community life to quantified monetary values. Just as, in the process of alienation, labour, life activity, becomes transformed into a mere commodity, a means of exchange, so the individual himself becomes a commodity. Thus, in educational terms, students may be referred to as a 'pool of ability': the talents and productive abilities of people become regarded as resources to serve the economy, rather like natural mineral resources. They are not so much selected for different educational routes according to their suitability to maximise their developmental capacities, but rather are classified and graded on a one-dimensional scale of merit and reward. Some young people are 'university material', others are 'college of education' material, and still others are not suitable material for higher education. In this way, people are graded rather like coal: some coal is labelled grade one, other coal receives a lower grade, and the poorest of all is thrown on the slag-heap. In the labour market, the job seeker may be selling not only specific skills, but his personality as well. The right 'personality' can mean promotion, or a move to a better job. It may therefore be cultivated with this end in view, and thus becomes an object, viewed as a means of exchange.

The alienation of labour, then, does not refer to a narrow sphere of 'work' – as it is usually defined in opposition to other activities – but refers much more generally to the alienation of life activity. Douglas Holly[8] has shown how aspects of the educational process in British society are characterised by alienation, and it is worth considering his description here as it provides a very good illustration of the concept as it has been presented here. Holly embraces a humanistic conception of education, seeing it as 'personal development and fulfilment and the full realisation of human potential'.[9] On the other hand, 'alienated education can be seen as the educational process externalised, made instrumental instead of expressive and self realising'.[10] Where education is instrumental it is conceived of as a means of obtaining qualifications for the purpose of career advancement: thus the sixth-form course may be geared entirely to 'A'-level examinations. The students may be given frequent tests to develop examination technique, and aspects of the subject which need not be studied for the examination, however great their intrinsic interest, are ignored: to study them would be wasting time, for the success of the teacher is judged in terms of the examination results. In the humanistic view, the educational process is the life activity of the student, but conceived instrumentally, it becomes merely a means to existence, the securing of paper qualifications in order to obtain future material rewards. Humanistically, the process of education represents the development of a relationship between the individual and the natural world: knowledge realises the potential of the individual and as such is part of the individual's self. Usually, however, education is seen as something external, which is acquired; subjects are there to be learnt, and appropriate pieces of them to be reproduced in examinations. Education thus becomes transformed from a relationship into an external, and therefore alien, object. The student who reads a book in order to be able to reproduce its contents in an examination does not experience his activity of reading as intrinsic to himself but as an alien activity. Very likely, he will assess his effort by something like the number of pages he has read. An 'education', as an object that is acquired which can be exploited in the job market, becomes a commodity, valued in monetary exchange terms.

Holly's description of alienation in education helps to clarify two sources of confusion in the use of the concept, these being its associations with *feelings* of alienation, and with involvement.

It may seem that to say that an individual experiences his activity as an alien activity is much the same as saying that he *feels* alienated. Thus, sociologists studying factories may measure alienation in terms of whether workers feel alienated from their work, whether they are bored, dissatisfied, or feel that their work is meaningless to them. Using this notion of alienation in the educational sphere, we might say that the secondary modern 'C'-streamer, who has no interest in school academic activities, who is only there because he has to be, and whose main interest in the classroom is to avoid work and cause disruption, is alienated from education. A study by David Hargreaves provides some apt statements by such pupils.

> 'I copy off (X). He couldn't stop me cos I'd smash him and take the book.'
> 'Our class (4D) is better than 4C. You get a better laugh. We throw rubbers at Mr X———.'
> 'I work one lesson, and you know, try to do as much as I can. Then I don't do nowt and I just keep putting the dates about every three sums. And you get away with it.'[11]

There can be little doubt that this is a form of alienation from education. However, Holly's description is concerned as much with the bright and studious grammar school pupil who is praised by his teachers who wants good 'A'-levels so that he can go to a prestigious university. He may be quite happy at school, and not feel alienated in any way, but if he experiences his education as an external and instrumental activity, then it may be said that he is alienated. It could even be said that alienation is more extreme in this case than for the member of the secondary modern 4D who enjoys throwing rubbers at his hapless teacher. In the latter case, education is alienative, but it does not perhaps occupy a very significant part of the boy's life activity; he might be fascinated by motor engines, and spend much of his out-of-school time working on them, totally engrossed. The would-be Oxbridge student, on the other hand, might well spend most of his spare time doing 'homework', learning and revising for his examinations. For him education is not only alienative, but it also dominates his life activity. So it can be seen that if an activity is alienative, then it may be said that the greater is the involvement in the activity, the greater is the alienation. The idea that alienation is greater where people are not involved in their activities is therefore quite false. The notion of the clock-watching assembly-line car-worker as an extreme case of alienation in modern society, frequently conjured up by middle-class sociologists, is quite misleading. Extreme instances of alienation in the occupational sphere are more likely to be found among professional occupations. The academic who is totally involved in the production of academic work, and whose other life activities are subordinated to it so that he can write as many books and papers as possible and thereby secure preferment, status and recognition, is surely more alienated than the car-worker because virtually his whole life activity is instrumental and externalised.

To return now to the question of placing alienation in the context of role language, it has been noted above that people are alienated when they do not identify with the roles they play. In alienated role playing, where the individual is alienated from his activities, it may appear that the role is estranged from the self. Thus, the person who is frustrated in his occupation may proclaim that 'this is not really me'. However, it was suggested in Chapter 4 (p. 84) that the individual's experience of himself is derived from the roles he plays. It would therefore seem that the Marxian concept of alienation is not compatible with the framework of role analysis developed in Chapter 4. Though there are considerable difficulties, this is not necessarily so. It may be that the individual is estranged from himself in one or more roles while identifying with himself in other roles. Thus, the alienated salesman is only too well aware that he *is* a salesman: other people see him as a salesman, and his view of himself derives from the reflections of others. Yet, in that he does not see himself as 'being himself' in the salesman role, he is alienated from himself in that particular role. Instead, he identifies with the selves he derives from his other roles. Thus alienated role playing may thus be seen as self-estrangement.

Difficulties arise if we are faced with an individual who is characterised by total alienation, who is estranged from himself in every role he plays. Here it would seem that the individual's self derives from something other than the roles he plays. Yet such a situation represents not the estrangement of the individual's experience of himself from his roles, but rather the estrangement of both his roles and his experience of himself from an ideal conception of his true nature, his species being in Marxian terms. It is not the individual's conception and experience of himself that is independent of his roles: it is not possible for a person to experience or have a conception of himself that is independent of his activities. Rather, the individual is estranged from the sociologist's conception of his ideal nature that is represented neither in that person's self nor in the roles he plays. The totally alienated person will surely have an alienated conception of himself corresponding to his roles: if he acts as a machine, or a puppet in all his roles, then he may well see himself as a machine or puppet. The moneylender who is totally engrossed in pecuniary accumulation need experience no estrangement of self from role: yet in the Marxian conception of alienation, he is clearly alienated: his whole life activity is devoted to the accumulation of the means of exchange, and all is subordinated to abstract monetary values.

To avoid confusion, a distinction must be made between the alienation of individuals who do not identify with particular roles that they play and thereby experience some estrangement between role and self, and the alienation of the individual in his activities from some ideal conception of human nature. In the first case, while the individual may not regard himself as alienated, he does have some experience which corresponds to alienation: he perceives that he is 'not his real self' in a particular role. In the second case, it is the sociologist who judges the individual to be dehumanised, alienated from his species being in his life activities. Implications of this distinction will be considered further in the concluding section of this chapter.

Role playing may also be seen as alienated where the individual takes his role as an external object, laid out by society, into which he must fit. Here, the role player is taking his own activities not as part of himself but as subject to external control. Because roles may be located in the structure of society, and as such are at least in part determined by the structure of society, it may be thought that role playing inevitably tends to be alienative. Yet when it is said that roles are located in the structure of society, what is meant is that they can be seen only in the context of social relationships, relationships between people in which individuals create and modify their conceptions of their roles and the roles of others. Alienation is present when roles are played as if they were set out and controlled by society as objective and external entities. Berger and Luckmann have described how the social world, the world of social institutions, although a product of human activity confronts the individual as an external, objective reality.[12] They also note a tendency for the social world to be seen as not only outside the individual, but beyond his control. Phenomena of human relationships are thus seen as non-human things: in this way politicians may talk about the needs of 'the economy' as if this is some non-human system that dictates their actions. This process, whereby the relationships between people become conceived as things is described by Berger and Luckmann, following Marx, as reification,[13] and is another facet of alienation: where roles and social relationships become reified, they become dehumanised. Roles are reified when they are treated merely as external tasks which the individual is required to perform. The occupational role that the individual takes and conforms to as a means to material subsistence alone is thus reified. If the role requires 'personality', as in the case of the salesman, then the individual's self also becomes reified, treated by its possessor and employers alike as a thing, a commodity, to be manipulated and bartered for profit. C. Wright Mills has thus described the reification of the self of the salesgirl:

> In the normal course of her work, because her personality becomes the instrument of an alien purpose, the salesgirl becomes self-alienated. In one large department store, a planted observer said of one girl: 'I have been watching her for three days now. She wears a fixed smile on her made-up face, and it never varies, no matter to whom she speaks. I never heard her laugh spontaneously or naturally. Either she is frowning or her face is devoid of any expression. When a customer approaches, she immediately assumes her hard, forced smile. It amazes me, because although I know that the smiles of most salesgirls are unreal, I've never seen such calculation given to the timing of a smile. I myself tried to copy such an expression, but I am unable to keep such a smile on my face if it is not sincerely and genuinely motivated'.[14]

If the individual does not identify with a reified role, then he experiences self-estrangement from that particular role. Reification of the self, however, represents estrangement of self from the sociologist's conception of the nature of man, its dehumanisation.

It follows from what has been said that the conformist who plays the role laid out for him, and who sees that he has no control over it, is alienated. Now it may be that some individuals appear to conform in their roles while they are not particularly bothered about conforming: sober and highly conventional clothing may indicate that the wearer is concerned about activities other than dress, rather than conformist attitudes. It may be said, though, that the individual whose prime orientation in role playing is conformity is alienated in that role: he is not expressing himself in that particular role, and his approach is purely instrumental. There is therefore no reason to assume that the deviant is any more alienated than the conformist, though it must not be thought that the argument here implies that the reverse is the case, that the deviant is less likely to be alienated than the conformist. The opposite of alienation is freedom, and conformity is associated with alienation because of its association with lack of freedom. Deviance does not necessarily imply freedom any more than conformity, as will be seen in the discussion of deviance below.

If treating roles as things to be used instrumentally is alienation, then it might seem that the use of techniques of impression management (already discussed on pp. 86–91) indicates alienation in role playing. This is certainly the case where the individual projects an image of self which he knows to be false in order to take advantage of others, where the motor-car salesman, for example, affects genuine concern for the welfare of his customer so that the latter will lose his guard and be sold a worthless vehicle. Impression management, however, is a basic requirement for the process of communication in role playing. It is through impression management that the individual is creative in his role and exercises control over his situation. As a requirement for self-expression in human communication, there is no necessary connection between impression management and alienation.

Taking yet another aspect of role playing discussed above (pp. 96–100), it might be assumed that role distance signifies alienation. For by taking role distance, the individual signifies to himself and others that he is something other than the role he plays, and that his self is not, at least not altogether, to be identified with the role that he is playing. Alienation, it has been said, can be defined in terms of lack of identification of the individual with his roles. It is possible to conceive of instances where role distance is clearly indicative of alienation, as when the castle guide manages to convey in his commentary to tourists that the castle has no intrinsic interest for him and that he is only giving the commentary because he has to. Generally, however, role distance implies that the individual is not totally absorbed by, not totally involved in his given role in the situation. It has been noted above that it is mistaken to associate involvement necessarily with the absence of alienation. In taking role distance, the individual is allowing other elements of his self, derived from playing his other roles, to creep into his performance. He is being himself and expressing himself, rather than compartmentalising himself in his role. There is no intrinsic reason why the surgeon who cracks jokes during an operation, or the committee man who doodles, should be regarded as alienated. As a creative element in role playing, role distance may thus signify the absence of alienation more frequently than its presence.

THE SOCIAL DEFINITION OF DEVIANCE

Deviance is most simply defined as conduct which is not in accordance with social norms, and it follows from this that without social norms there could be no deviance. It is society, through social norms, that defines deviance, and thus deviance as a sociological concept can be seen to derive from the perspective of 'society'. It is an elementary lesson of sociology that moral and immoral standards of behaviour can be judged only in relation to the social norms of the society in which they occur. The acquisition of two wives may be socially approved conduct in one society, but criminal deviance in another. Stealing can occur only in societies which recognise private ownership of property. Indeed, property as a term does not simply refer to objects, but rather describes a social relationship – the rights of individuals in relation to other people with respect to objects. Deviance is thus not inherent in any particular action, but is socially defined. Just as a particular action may be deviant in one society and not in another, so it may or may not be deviant in any one society according to the social setting and situation in which it takes place. Thus in Britain a schoolteacher is allowed to beat children in his charge, and in Scotland he is even provided with a belt by his employers for this very purpose. Similar action by bus conductors, or even policemen, could result in criminal prosecution for assault. In certain social circles drunkenness late on Saturday evening might be acceptable, whereas it would not be at Thursday lunchtime. Deviance may be seen as likely to occur in social settings where attachment to social norms is somewhat weak. Thus, as noted in Chapter 2 (p. 49) sociologists sometimes use the term *anomie* to describe such situations. Theories developed around the concept of *anomie* will be considered below as explanations of deviance. Generally, however, it is a mistake to see deviance simply in terms of non-conformity to norms. As suggested in Chapter 3 (p. 72) the deviant is often not someone who just fails to conform to particular standards, but rather someone who chooses for himself standards that are different from those of most other people. Thus the hippie, who in terms of conventional norms is lazy, work-shy and simply 'living for kicks', is not someone who fails to live up to these norms, but someone who chooses a different set of standards, standards by which 'work' in the conventional sense is not a particularly virtuous activity. Thus it has been suggested that deviants may be people whose reference groups are different from conventionally accepted ones.

One further observation on the basic social definition of deviance can be made at this point. Socially defined deviance is only marginally related to statistical deviations from the average. Very short or very fat people are not deviants *per se*, neither are record-breaking athletes or exceptionally bosomy young ladies. There is, however, some relationship between social deviance and deviations from statistically average characteristics, because of the tendency, discussed in Chapter 2, for things as they are to come to be regarded as things as they ought to be. The person of mixed or changing sex is a social deviant because people *ought* to be men and women. Erving Goffman[15] has well described how physical deformities result in individuals becoming socially stigmatised. The stigma the deformed and crippled carry is not the stigma of physical deformity so much as that of the social reaction to their deformity. It may seem that such people are stigmatised because of their horrible appearance, as in the tragic example used by Goffman for the frontispiece of his book:

> ... I would like to have boy friends like the other girls and go out on Saturday nites, but no boy will take me because I was born without a nose. . . .
> I sit and look at myself all day and cry. I have a big hole in the middle of my face that scares people even myself so I can't blame boys for not wanting to take me out. My mother loves me, but she crys terrible when she looks at me.[16]

In general, though, stigmatised people are those who for some reason or other fail to meet acceptable standards of normality, and the stigmas indicating that they are not normal may be social as well as physical:

thus the homosexual and ex-convict are stigmatised as well as the physically deformed. More will be said of stigmas below. They have been introduced here to indicate the connexion between socially defined deviance and deviation from statistical normality. Of course, what is defined as normal in society is relative to the social norms of that society. There can be no absolute standard of normality.

In the context of role playing, the deviant may be someone who fails to meet the expectations attached to his roles. From the point of view of role theory, all deviance could be seen as deviance in role performance. This enables us to locate deviance in specific roles, and perhaps within particular sectors of roles played by individuals. Thus the defence of the embezzler will at his trial refer to his fine record of military service, and his devotion to church and youth work in the hope of reducing the sentence of the court. Acceptable and praiseworthy role performances are publicised in the hope of mitigating the penalty for the one glaring deviant role performance. Such a defence may well be advisable because of the tendency of the deviant label to be applied universally to the criminal, so that he is seen to be generally deviant, rather than deviant in the context of one specific role performance. Thus gypsies, whose deviance consists of their choosing to live in mobile caravans rather than houses, are generally considered to be dirty, lazy and dishonest as well. Young men who sport exceptionally long hair are frequently considered to be immoral and to possess other undesirable characteristics. In this context, we may note the contents of a letter from a fund-giving foundation to the Vice-Chancellor of Warwick University:

> I was very interested to see round this wonderful new University and how glad I was to see the fruits of British workmanship in such excellent buildings.
>
> However, I cannot say that I was impressed by your students; how sad it is to see these long-haired louts wearing jeans and sandals flopping around in such splendid surroundings. What a pity you cannot order them to wear some sort of uniform – if only a cap and gown.[17]

Not all deviance should be seen as deviance *from* role expectations, because some forms of deviance occur as the performance of deviant roles. The prostitute and professional burglar are deviant roles, which will largely be played in the context of a deviant community. There are other types of deviant roles, which are deviant in the context of the social group in which they are played. These would include the village idiot, the classroom troublemaker, and the office clown. Such individuals are expected to deviate from the norms of the social groups to which they belong, though they are still accepted as group members. Goffman refers to such deviant role performers as in-group deviants, distinguishing them from social deviants who are members of deviant communities and isolated deviants.[18] It should be noted that social pressures and expectations tend to confirm the deviant role player in his deviance. Once the clerk has been defined as the office clown, it is very difficult for him to escape from this role. In rather different ways, the prostitute and professional burglar will not find it easy to discard their deviant roles and acquire 'straight' ones. Social groups reinforce the deviance of their in-group deviants, just as deviant communities reinforce the deviance of their members. In the case of deviant communities, deviance may be reinforced by other groups as well who will not accept the individual who seeks to leave the deviant community. The unsuccessful convicted burglar will always be a prominent suspect in the investigation of future burglaries, and receiving so much police attention it will be difficult for him to avoid further court appearances should the police believe these to be desirable.

The social definition of deviance is not simply a process of the recognition of social norms and the observations of infractions of these norms, but a vastly more complex and in many ways haphazard process. The individualistic perspective, focusing on the perception and actions of individuals, must now contribute to the discussion. First of all, by no means all deviance will be socially observed. If we take infractions of criminal law, the number of crimes known to the police will constitute only a fraction of the actual number of criminal acts. There is really no means of telling just what proportion of crimes committed appears in police statistics, though it is possible to point to some of the factors at work affecting the probability of a criminal act becoming a crime known to the police. One factor is the probability of the crime being reported to the police. 'Victimless' crimes, such as certain types of sexual offences, and drug offences, are unlikely to be reported, and it is likely that the incidence of such acts is infinitely greater than the number known to the police. Another basic factor in the translation of criminal acts into crimes known to the police is the patterning of police activity. It would be quite impossible for the police to devote all the necessary resources to the detection of every type of crime, and thus there is a tendency to select particular types of crime for intensive detection work. Different police forces may focus their energies on different sorts of crime, one perhaps paying special attention to drug offences, another to homosexual offences, and perhaps a third to under-age drinking and other licensing law infringements. Variations in rates for different sorts of crime between police areas may thus be a reflection more of different sorts of police activity than of variations in actual criminal activity. Rises and falls in crime rates, too, may be largely unrelated to changes in patterns of criminal activity, but produced by changes in patterns of police activity. Jock Young has described how a fantasy crime wave may be manufactured by the press and the police.

> As the mass media fan up public indignation over marihuana use, pressure on the police increases: the public demands that they solve the drug problem. The number of marihuana users known to the police is . . . a mere tip of the iceberg of actual smokers. The police, then, given their desire to enact public opinion and legitimise their position, will act with greater vigilance and arrest more marihuana offenders. All that happens is that they dig deeper into the undetected part of the iceberg, the statistics for marihuana soar; the public, the press and the magistrates view the new figures with even greater alarm. Increased pressure is put on the police, the latter dig even deeper into the iceberg and the figures increase once again, public concern becoming even greater. We have entered into what I term a fantasy crime wave which does not necessarily involve at any time an actual increase in the number of marihuana smokers.[19]

Just as police activity may be focused on particular types of crimes to the neglect of others, so it may also be concentrated on particular social groups and particular areas of the police district. In cities, police activity may be concentrated on the poorer working-class districts to the neglect of the more affluent middle-class areas. Crime may well be less visible in the leafy middle-class suburb, with its inhabitants secluded in privacy, than in the more closely packed working-class district. Gypsies are much more vulnerable to prosecution for motoring offences than are middle-class commuters.

Deviant activities do not therefore automatically translate themselves into socially recognised and labelled deviance, and a number of social processes must be considered in explaining what sorts of deviance become thus recognised and labelled. The process of detection and observation of deviance is only one aspect of the problem, because it is not simply that some deviant acts are secret and unobserved, whereas others are detected. This would imply that social norms, including criminal laws, are so clear cut that any deviant act that is observed can immediately be classified as deviant or otherwise. This may sometimes be so: the passer-by in the street who observed someone hurl a brick through a shop window and then proceed to remove its contents clearly has little difficulty in deciding that he has witnessed a deviant and criminal act. However, deviance is by no means always so unambiguous, and the recognition of deviance may be dependent upon processes of decision-making as to whether particular acts are deviant, and whether the individuals who commit them are to be regarded as deviants. These two sorts of decision-making are by no means the same.

It may be possible for an individual to commit a number of deviant acts without himself being labelled as a deviant. Minor eccentricities are likely to be tolerated, but if they become major, at some point in time the individual will be defined as mentally ill. His deviance has reached the threshold of social recognition. The business executive may have his minor excesses in the rendering of his expense accounts overlooked, but again, when they exceed a certain level he will be regarded as a deviant, and penalties will be incurred. The amount of deviance that is tolerated before the threshold of social labelling as a deviant is crossed will vary according to the social circumstances and position of the individual. A senior politician indulging in frequent bouts of drunkenness in the House of Commons will keep his position far longer than a filing clerk in the House engaging in similar behaviour. The business executive may be permitted far greater appropriations from the firm through expense account excesses than those of the storeman of the firm through removal of stock. In all these cases there is a threshold beyond which further deviant acts lead to the individual being classified as a deviant.

Whether any particular act is regarded as deviant depends on a decision by the observer, and perhaps by the actor too, as to whether what has happened should be regarded as deviant. Thus, Dennis Chapman describes a series of events on a building site in an upper middle-class suburb.

Each evening and every weekend, after the workmen had departed, the site was visited by between five or fifteen men with motor-cars or wheelbarrows. They removed bricks, tiles, paving slabs, timber, mortar, and other building materials systematically, and often in large quantities. (The builder estimated his losses as between 5 and 10 per cent of the total.) It was possible to identify them and classify them by occupation; they were all in the Registrar General's occupational Groups I and II (professional and managerial).

On one occasion when a patrolling policeman was present, the observer asked him why he did not intervene. The policeman's reply was that he assumed that they all had had permission. Even though the site was visited on many occasions by the police, no one was questioned at any time.[20]

Aaron Cicourel, in a study of juvenile delinquency, has described how juvenile delinquents are produced and processed by the system of juvenile justice.[21] The classification of young people as delinquents is dependent upon the decision of policeman and probation officers as to whether what happened was delinquency. Such a decision will be influenced by such things as whether the potential delinquent has a 'bad' attitude, whether he comes from a 'good' – usually middle-class – family, or whether he comes from a 'broken' home. 'Bad' attitudes, 'good' families and 'broken' homes are not objective criteria with standard and unambiguous meanings but subjective assessments arrived at in particular situations in terms of the routine everyday expectations of policemen and probation officers. Cicourel thus sees crime statistics not as objective indices of the incidence of criminal activities in society, but as something produced through the routine everyday decision-making of agencies responsible for coping with crime. The high proportion of working-class offenders in the statistics on juvenile delinquency is to be seen in these terms: working-class teenagers are more likely to have 'bad' attitudes and less likely to come from 'good' families.

At the beginning of this chapter the idea that deviance be regarded as some sort of pathological manifestation was dismissed. It was Emile Durkheim who pointed out that deviance was an inherent feature of the organisation of society. Crime, he suggested, was normal. In any society, infractions from social norms would occur: even in the most moral society, some would be more moral than others, and what might seem to the outsider to be minor misdemeanours would be defined as heinous crimes.[22] Regarding crime as normal in contrast to the conventional view of crime as pathological, Durkheim went on to suggest, that far from serving solely to disrupt society, crime actually contributed positively to the social order. Social norms would be reinforced by the expression of common sentiments against crime and criminals. Following Durkheim, the function of the trial, the public branding, literally or otherwise, and punishment of the criminal is not his reform, but the affirmation of and thereby reinforcement of common sentiments and attachment to social norms. Crime reporting, especially of the more villainous and lurid crimes, is a major activity of the popular press, the modern equivalent of the medieval stocks. Expression of righteous indignation against and revulsion from the criminal reaffirms the individual's own membership of the moral community, while labelling the criminal as outside this community. The criminal is beyond the pale of the good society: he is the scapegoat, the stereo-typical villain. As Dennis Chapman has put it:

> Originally the lowest and most deprived group in feudal society (except for the slave), villains have in their stereotyped symbolic form continued to represent the evil concentrated in the lowest social groups. . . . Associated with the stereotype are elaborations, mainly discarded by the criminologist but still affecting popular thinking and social action, that criminals and other socially pathological persons are physically, psychologically, or racially inferior, or – a recent variation – members of a cultural sub-group: the racial theory reborn in modern anthropological language.[23]

As a stereotyped scapegoat, the criminal is drawn from the lowest status groups in society, and in a class-stratified society, such as Britain, the criminal is located in the working class. Chapman shows how the activities of the police and the courts, and the reporting of crime in the press, all serve to perpetuate the stereotype of the criminal as a member of the working class. Various social processes serve to confer relative immunity on members of the middle and upper classes from being apprehended and publicly labelled as criminals. A large area of 'white-collar crime' – crimes peculiar to the upper and middle classes – such as falsifying tax returns, offences against the Factories Act and against the Food and Drugs Acts, offences which are known to be frequent, are rarely the subject of police action. People who are caught in attempts to avoid paying income tax are usually privately fined by the Inland Revenue Commissioners, and rarely appear in criminal courts. Public-school boys are almost never juvenile delinquents because, even if apprehended in criminal activities by the police, they will usually be handed over to their headmaster for treatment, rather than be brought before the courts.

If the middle-class criminal is unfortunate enough to be brought before the courts, his treatment is likely to be different from that of the working-class criminal fitting the stereotype. If his crime is an 'ordinary' one – one fitting the working-class stereotype – then attempts may be made to show that he does not in fact fit the stereotype. Chapman provides numerous examples from the press. Of an accountant who stole wallets from his colleagues, the defence was as follows:

> Mr Bell said there was no reason for Mr X to commit such an offence. He had been examined by psychiatrists who had stated that the offence was due to the state of his health.[24]

For an ex-public-school girl who stole a cheque book and obtained goods by false pretences:

> Mr Frere said she came to London alone. She 'got in with a thoroughly bad set of layabouts'.
> . . . .
> Arrangements had now been made for her to live with a vicar and his wife in the West Country.[25]

Where the offender is charged with a specifically 'white-collar crime', even in very serious cases, the penalty is usually a fine. Chapman again provides many intriguing examples, and compares the case of a thirty-six-year-old company director fined £1,500 for taking part in a £31,920 purchase tax fraud with a building site clerk, sent to prison for twelve months for stealing £5 from his employers.[26]

That crime appears largely as a working-class phenomenon is not because working-class people are more likely to possess criminal natures than other social classes, but because of the social processes that produce crime and criminals, particularly the routine decision-making of those agencies concerned with the processing of crime and criminals – notably the police and the courts. More generally, it could be said that if the incidence of deviance is higher in some social groups than others, explanation is to be sought not by asking why particular sorts of people are deviant in their activities but why they come to be regarded as deviant. Deviant activities, in themselves, are a very general and widespread feature of social life, and not confined only to certain sorts of people or certain sorts of social groups. This point may be illustrated by reference to Goffman's work on stigmas. People who are stigmatised are defined as being other than normal: either by physical personal attributes, or because of some events in their past, the identity of stigmatised individuals is spoiled. Some causes of stigmatisation, such as physical deformities or speech defects, cannot be concealed, and will be immediately apparent to all, but often the individual is able to control the discrediting information about himself, and 'pass' as a normal person. Thus the ex-convict may conceal his prison record from his workmates, and the wife of the mental patient conceal that her husband is in fact a mental patient. Goffman describes vividly the intricate techniques whereby people who are discreditable but not discredited keep their skeletons locked in their cupboards. But it should not be thought that these are techniques required of and practised only by an unfortunate minority.

> . . . stigma involves not so much a set of concrete individuals who can be separated into two piles, the stigmatised and the normal, as a pervasive two-role social process in which every individual participates in both roles, at least in some connexions and in some phases of life. The normal and the stigmatized are not persons but perspectives.[27]

Everyone is potentially discreditable in terms of some aspect of his assumed character. Similarly, it may be suggested that everyone is, in some of the roles he plays during some stages of his life, a deviant. Deviance relates very closely to stigma in that deviance is stigmatising: information about the deviance of an individual has the potential of discrediting him. Much of the discussion of deviance here has been focused on crime, the infractions of criminal law, and just as everyone is deviant at some time or other during his life, so also everyone is probably a criminal in some activity sometime during his life. Indeed, it is not uncommon for celebrities to disclose in interviews or autobiographies at a late stage of their lives their own juvenile delinquencies. Such information is no longer discrediting. Even so, it may still sound either extremely cynical, or merely absurd, and probably both, to make such a bold statement as to the universality of criminality. Such a reaction, however, is a product of the common-sense definition of a world in which criminals are set apart from law-abiding citizens, and, to a lesser extent, deviants from ordinary decent people. Criminals and non-criminals are not perspectives: in a real sense they are concrete individuals, separated into two piles! But the separation process is a social one, which produces and labels some individuals as criminals, and is not a classification based on objectively defined criteria.

It is not within the scope of this book to present here a critique, or even a brief summary, of the various sociological theories that are current as explanations of deviance. Some of the implications of our discussion on the nature of deviance are, however, worth pointing out. If deviance is regarded as socially produced in the very broad sense outlined above, it follows that, in order to explain why the incidence of deviance appears higher in some social groups than in others, the problem that must be addressed is why members of particular social groups are more likely to be produced and labelled as deviants than others, rather than that of why some people are more likely to engage in deviant activities than others. One theory which tends to take the latter approach is *anomie* theory. *Anomie* generally can be taken to mean a social condition in which attachment to the normative order is weak. Robert K. Merton, in formulating his *anomie* theory,[28] presents *anomie* as a condition of the social structure in which there is some disjunction between culturally approved values and culturally approved means of obtaining these values. *Anomie* occurs where excessive emphasis is placed on the one at the expense of the other: emphasis on cultural values may be such that any means whether legitimate or not, will be sought to achieve them. The emphasis in society on 'monetary success', for example, may be such that there tends to be little attention paid to whether this success is achieved by legitimate or deviant means. For some social groups, the possibility of achieving the cultural values – success – by culturally approved means may be much less than for others. Merton, writing in the 1950s, cites the American Dream: the belief that everyone should strive to 'get ahead', and that everyone has the opportunity to do so by hard work. He suggests that *anomie* is characteristic of American society in that the emphasis is placed on success, rather than on whether the means of achieving it are legitimate. Opportunities for 'getting ahead' and 'monetary success' are not equally distributed, and thus pressures are exerted particularly on the lower strata of society, whose legitimate opportunities are very circumscribed: 'hard work' might achieve much for the son of a corporation president, but probably very little for a Harlem slum boy. Hence we have an explanation of the higher incidence of deviant behaviour among the lower social strata of society. Merton's theory is much more sophisticated than it has been possible to indicate here, and his theory is a most important contribution to the sociology of deviance. However, in so far as it attempts to explain differential rates of deviant behaviour across different social groups, it is unsatisfactory. Criminal statistics, as suggested above, are not adequate as evidence that criminal deviance is higher among lower-class groups than the rest of the population. It is not primarily the differential incidence of deviant activities that requires explanation. One American study,[29] following Merton's approach, has suggested that conditions of *anomie* are no more evident among lower-class than among middle-class groups. The study revealed 'getting ahead' to be a very common value, but whereas lower-class people were found to define this in terms of material 'success' (concrete material rewards), middle-class people tended to define it in terms of less tangible achievements – status and social recognition. Thus, while a manual worker might see success in terms of owning his house, a good income, and a car, the professional person is more likely to see achievement in terms of the development of his professional status. Achievement is much more demanding than mere material success, and thus the study found that the gap between aspirations and expectations – what people thought they ought to achieve as opposed to what they thought they would – was as high for middle-class as for working-class people. *Anomie* is thus shown to be unsatisfactory as an explanation for class differences in deviant behaviour, though it may still provide a useful explanation of deviant behaviour *per se*.

ALIENATION AND DEVIANCE

Anomie theory provides a starting point for drawing together the connexions between alienation and deviance. Some studies in fact attempted to show empirically how alienation and *anomie* are associated,[30] though on close examination this association may turn out to be something of a tautology based on verbal confusion: *feelings* of *anomie* are related to *feelings* of alienation, and there may be little difference between them. For example, if people feel that they cannot control their fate, they may be described as anomic, and if they feel powerless, they may be regarded as alienated. Perhaps in both cases they would more appropriately be regarded as fatalistic. Clearly, there is little to be gained from this sort of approach. If we return to Merton's *anomie* theory, and his depiction of the dominant cultural values in the United States, then a direct relationship may be shown between alienation and deviance. If the dominant goals in an individual's life activity are the achievement of financial success or high social status, then life activity becomes merely instrumental to achieve these ends, and the individual is alienated in his activity. Life activity has become merely a means to existence. In gearing his life activity to the acquisition of material objects, such things as a new house, a new car or a colour television, these objects become the end to which the individual's activities are directed, rather than a means by which he relates the world and his activities to himself. Life activity is subordinated to and used for the acquisition of material objects. If the excessive emphasis on the culturally approved goal of material success at the expense of socially prescribed means represents the social condition of *anomie*, it is the choice of goals in the first place that signifies alienation. Deviance as a consequence of *anomie* may thus be dependent upon a prior state of alienation. The businessman whose commitment to profit and the expansion of his enterprise is such that he is prepared to flout the law and defraud his creditors to achieve his ends is such a deviant. His deviance reflects both the condition of *anomie* of the social order and the alienation of his own activities.

Even in this connexion, though, alienation and deviance are far from complementary. The bright working-class grammar-school boy who works hard for his exams, goes to university, then successfully works his way up the status ladder of a large industrial company, epitomises success and achievement by conformity. Yet, as suggested by the earlier discussion of alienation and education, his life activity, too, may be seen as a mere means to existence, and as such, alienated.

Merton's theory of *anomie* is probably best known for his typology of adaptations to *anomie*. He distinguishes five modes of adaptation: the conformist, who, like our bright grammar-school boy, seeks success by hard work; the innovator, who seeks material success by deviant means, as does the business racketeer; the ritualist, who has forgotten about success and is only concerned with conformity to petty rules and regulations, as might be true of the minor bureaucrat; the retreatist, who has opted out altogether, as has the tramp or the junkie: finally, the rebel, who, like the retreatest, rejects both the culturally approved success goals and the approved ways of achieving them, but, unlike the retreatist, positively defines for himself alternative values and standards of behaviour, as does the committed revolutionary. All adaptations other than conformity are deviant, though it may be argued that the ritualist, who appears to all as an over-conformist, is hardly deviant. The categories of the innovator and the rebel are the ones that concern us here, because they in particular throw light upon the relationship between alienation and deviance.

The innovator fits the stereotype of the criminal very well: he is not someone who openly challenges particular laws, and probably does not even disapprove of them in principle: he merely hopes to be able to evade them for his own personal advantage. Merton describes such a deviant as aberrant,[31] and distinguishes him from the non-conformist who openly challenges social norms, as does the rebel. Yet the appearance of the criminal as an aberrant deviant may turn out to be a function of the social processes producing deviance. If conviction seems likely, it may be more prudent for the criminal to be penitent, to claim that he has been foolish, misguided or ill in his 'moment of folly', to distinguish his moral self from his particular criminal action, than to identify himself with that action and say he thinks the law is silly. Jock Young thus describes the dilemma of the marihuana user:

> ... if the individual found in possession of marihuana actually finds himself in the courts he will find himself in a difficult position, namely that if he tells the truth and says that he smokes marihuana because he likes it, and because it does no harm and that therefore the law is wrong, he will receive a severe sentence. Whereas if he plays their game and conforms to their stereotype, namely that he had got into bad company, that somebody (the pusher) offered to sell him the stuff, so he thought he would try it out, that he knows he was foolish and won't do it again, the court will let him off lightly.[32]

Now if the deviant does accept the social definition of himself as deviant, then his deviance may be indicative of an acute form of alienation. For in such cases, the deviant does distinguish his moral self from his activities, which are then viewed, either through illness, weakness, or the effects of a drug to which he is addicted, as beyond his control. In the case of the convicted embezzler, the moral self is only distinguished from one particular set of acts in the individual's past. But in the case of the person who accepts the social definition of himself as mentally ill, virtually the whole self of the individual is defined as an object for therapeutic treatment. In the course of such treatment, the 'true self' with which the individual can identify is temporarily absent while it is being recast.

The non-conformist deviant, who identifies with and defends his activities which are socially defined as deviant, may be the least alienated of all. He chooses not to take for granted the social world nor accept the social roles that are laid out for him, but instead creates his own activity with which he can identify.

By viewing both alienation and deviance in the context of role playing, it can be seen quite clearly how these refer to quite different social phenomena. Deviance refers to the social assessment of whether the individual's conduct, his role playing, is in step with social expectations. Even where the individual defines himself as deviant, such a definition is a reflection upon other people's assessment of himself. Alienation, however, is not socially defined. Unlike deviance, alienation is not recognised in everyday language: for it is not society, but the sociologist who is the judge of whether an individual is alienated. The sociologist's description of people as alienated does not depend upon whether they feel alienated.

Alienation in role playing occurs when the individual does not identify himself with a particular role. Here, alienation corresponds to some experience the individual has of himself. The crucial factor is not whether his associates, his significant others, or 'society' accepts that he is 'really himself' in his role, but his own experience. Alienation used in this way might seem to refer only to a psychological state – the individual's feelings – but this is not the case. First of all, what the individual sees as 'really himself', though not represented in a particular role, is nevertheless socially derived, a product of his activities in his other roles. Secondly, it is the sociologist, and not the person he is studying, who describes the failure of the individual to express himself in a role as alienation. In applying such a description, the sociologist makes a moral judgement. The motor-car assembly-line worker may be only too well aware that he does not express himself in his work, but may regard the high pay as adequate compensation. It is the sociologist who judges that he is alienated in his work, and thereby makes the value judgement that the individual ought to express himself in his work.

The moral judgement of the sociologist is much more explicit where alienation describes the alienation of self from some ideal conception of the nature of man. The description of an individual as alienated in this way, such as C. Wright Mills' description of the reification of the self of the salesgirl, embodies a moral judgement on the quality of such an individual's life, that he is dehumanised. In presenting such descriptions, the sociologist embarks upon a moral critique of society. Thus Marx, in discussing capitalism in terms of alienation, embarks upon a moral critique of capitalism. Holly, in describing education in terms of alienation, embarks upon a moral critique of educational processes in British society. Following the Marxian tradition, it has been suggested that alienation should be seen as the opposite of freedom, freedom in the positive sense of self-realisation. The sociologist who thus employs the concept of alienation makes a moral judgement on the basis of commitment to this value of freedom.

No other sociological concept discussed so far implies such a moral judgement. Thus, in analysing deviance, the sociologist may note that the deviant may be morally condemned by his fellows, but may detach himself from any moral judgement in his analysis. All the sociological concepts discussed so far may be derived from the influence of society, from social interaction, from the tensions between the individual and society. But, in applying alienation, the sociologist is no longer content to understand social reality by interpreting the influences of society and the actions and understandings of its members. He now imparts his own moral standpoint, and thus goes beyond the sociological perspectives set out in this book. Is the sociologist entitled to make such moral judgements? Are they compatible with a sociological perspective? These are questions that must be answered satisfactorily, otherwise it must be concluded that alienation must be rejected as a sociological concept. They relate, however, to fundamental issues which are beyond the scope of the discussion in this chapter, and will be considered in the concluding chapter.

6. Power and Social Inequality

The distribution of power and the spread of social inequality in any society are very closely related to each other. The unravelling of this relationship will involve discussion of the notions of authority, élites and social classes in society, together with a consideration of the role of ideology. The four preceding chapters have focused very largely on concepts relating to the individual in society. Here the intention is to place this discussion in the context of elements of the wider structure of society. So often, the realms of micro-sociology and macro-sociology, concerned with the social context of individual activities and relations between major social groups and institutions respectively, seem to be virtually divorced and independent of each other. Thus, for example, grass-roots political activity and the workings of major political institutions may appear as quite separate realms of the social world. Role playing in everyday life and the social class structure may also appear to be quite distinct and separate. Yet, as indicated in Chapter 1 (p. 27), the study of the routine activities of everyday life, the area of micro-sociology, is important, because it is on these that the larger scale structuring of society, the power structure and the class structure are based. This chapter is concerned to make this relationship explicit. The starting point will be an analysis of the basic concept of power. The discussion will then move to consider the relationship between power and authority, which in turn will lead to the examination of the role of ideology in the maintenance of power. This will bring us to the central topic of the chapter, the relationship between power, social classes and élites in society. The chapter will conclude with a discussion of democracy and equality.

THE CONCEPT OF POWER

Power, as Mao Tse-tung once said, grows out of the barrel of a gun. Thus power is sometimes seen as the physical base of the social order. The maintenance of society as a social system, as was suggested in

Chapter 1 (p. 21), may be seen to depend on the distribution of power in society. Social order, in this view, is dependent on the concentration of power in the hands of those who are its prime beneficiaries. The social order, as indicated in Chapter 3 (p. 56), is dependent on the way people define the social situation. Where there are discordant definitions, then the ones which will be dominant will be the ones held by powerful groups in society. Thus, the expert planner's definition of the problem of urban renewal will usually have more influence on the course of events than that of a residents' or tenants' association. The role player, faced with incompatible expectations, may be orientated to comply with those expectations backed up by the most powerful sanctions. The location of deviant and criminal groups in society can also be seen to be dependent on power, in that, as indicated in Chapter 5 (p. 123), the stereotype of the deviant and criminal will be drawn from the lower strata, the weaker groups in society. Power may provide relative immunity from the process whereby deviants and criminals are produced and labelled. Alienation is intrinsically related to power, in that the alienation of the individual from his activities implies a lack of control over his activities. The alienated individual is subject to some force outside himself, whether it be in the more abstract form of the standards of 'monetary success' or in the more human form of his employer. Powerlessness has thus been seen as an essential dimension of alienation.[1]

Power thus appears as a significant determinant of many of the features of social phenomena discussed in previous chapters, but it is mistaken to see it as some sort of external, physical or material factor determining social relations. Power is not physical force, but refers fundamentally to a social relationship. Max Weber's definition of power, as 'the probability that one actor within a social relationship will be in a position to carry out his own will despite resistance',[2] is generally accepted by sociologists as a starting point for discussions of power in society. In this definition, the possession of power involves not simply the ability of the individual to control his own activities, but also to control the activities of others. Power in this sense is power of some people over others. In a more recent formulation, Peter Blau has conceived the power relationship as an exchange. In this view, power is exercised where an individual or social group requires something from another individual or social group, but has nothing equivalent to offer in return: the goods or services required may then only be obtained by the submission of the individual or social group to the power of those who control such goods and services.[3] This exchange may be illustrated at both interpersonal and group levels. In an unequal sexual relationship where, for instance, the boy is more strongly attracted to the girl than she is to him, the relationship may only be maintained by the boy being very submissive to the girl, and doing everything that she wants him to. The attractions to each other are not mutually balanced, and thus one party acquires power over the other in the continuance of the relationship. In feudal society, the serf received security and protection from the feudal lord in return for bondage, and in Victorian England the wage worker might receive bare subsistence and a hovel to live in, in return for twelve hours work a day. These are exchange relationships, because the serf and the worker, in theory at least, have the choice between submitting and absconding, or foregoing a wage, or taking part in a revolt or machine breaking. Blau is careful to emphasise that the conceptualisation of power relationships as a form of exchange should not be taken as a justification of power. The exchange may be very unequal, just as in the conventional economic sphere, an individual who has a monopoly over the distribution of an essential commodity is able to grossly inflate the price.

Sometimes sociologists distinguish between potential power, reputations of power, and the actual exercise of power. Thus, community power studies have found that while certain individuals in a community might be generally regarded as very powerful in that community, they might in fact not take part in, nor even seek to influence, the decision-making process in that community.[4] Arnold Rose has suggested that community studies which base their methods on asking who is powerful (who runs this town?) produce evidence not of the actual power structure, but of images of power.[5] Yet images of power and the actual exercise of power cannot really be regarded as distinct phenomena. As a social relation, the exercise of power depends upon its recognition by those subject to it. Sometimes, indeed, it may seem that people are powerful only because they are believed to be so, and for no other reason. Thus, in the local community, the possession of a reputation of power may result in the exercise of power if, as a result of such a reputation, an individual is consulted and asked for his opinions and advice. Conversely, the exercise of power by people who do have control over scarce resources will be severely limited if this power is not recognised. An industrialist will not be able to influence local government policies in his community by threatening to move his factory elsewhere, unless it is believed that he is willing and able to carry out his threat. It is true that if his threat is disregarded or not taken seriously, the industrialist can show the local politicians they were wrong and carry out the threat, but by doing so he will be abandoning the community. Power in the community, in this case, cannot be exercised unless it is recognised.

It follows from this discussion that it is a mistake to see power as some 'objective' factor in social relations, in comparison with the more 'subjective' ones, such as roles, reference groups and definitions of the situation.

From the basic proposition that power represents a social relation, three alternative propositions about the nature of power may be derived, each representing major theoretical approaches to the study of power in society. The first of these sees the exercise of power, the existence of dominance and subjection as an inherent feature of social organisation, just as we might regard social norms as an inherent feature of social organisation. One of the clearest statements of this position is given by Ralf Dahrendorf:

> ... authority is a type of social relation present in every conceivable social organisation. ...
> ... authority is a universal element of social structure. ...
> ... the existence of domination and subjection is a common feature of all possible types of authority and indeed, of all possible types of association and organisation.[6]

Here Dahrendorf is discussing a specific type of power – authority, which is power that is regarded as legitimate, and of which more must be said below. The more general point to be drawn here is that in this formulation power is an inherent feature of social relations and not a derivative of some other feature of social relations. From this conception of power in society it follows that conflict is also an inherent feature of social relations. Because social relations are characterised by dominance and subjection, there is always resistance to the exercise of power: the powerful groups in society are able to press their interests against those of the powerless, who will nevertheless seek to challenge the exercise of such power. For Dahrendorf, the exercise of power and the resistance to its exercise represent the fundamental dynamic feature of society in the production of social change.[7] The conception of power as an inherent feature of social relations is thus associated with what is

commonly regarded as the 'conflict theory' of society. This is sometimes, but quite wrongly, identified with Marxist theories. In fact, its
intellectual basis is to be found in the traditions of élite theory, developed largely as a critique of Marx,[8] and of liberalism. These connexions
cannot be explored here, though some discussion of élite theory is given
below (p. 142).

In both the remaining alternative conceptions of power, it is seen
not as an inherent feature of social organisation, but as a derivative of
some other aspect of social relations. In the one instance, power is seen
as a derivative of the normative order, the moral order of social life,
and is characteristic of what is broadly known as 'consensus theory'.
In the other, the Marxist conception, power is seen as derived from
productive activities, from the social relations involved in the means of
production. Each alternative merits separate discussion.

For those who like to think in twos, 'conflict' theory, corresponding
to the perspective of power and conflict, and 'consensus' theory,
corresponding to the social system perspective, represent the two
alternative frameworks for sociological analysis, and it is certainly the
case that in many respects they are diametrically opposed. In the
'conflict' view, with power as an inherent feature of social relations,
the normative order is seen as a derivative of the exercise of power.
Social norms are established and maintained in so far as they serve the
interests of the powerful. Whereas in the 'consensus' view, it is the
normative order that is the basis of social relations, and power that is
a derivative of this. It was a central theme of Chapter 2 that the social
order is a moral order, that society is ordered according to moral rules.
As a derivative of the normative order, power is seen primarily as conferred on people and exercised in accordance with the moral order.
Used in this way, power is seen primarily as a resource for the achievement of social goals, exercised in accordance with the social consensus,
the normative order. Now it might appear that such a conception of
power is obviously unsatisfactory, because it is not difficult to find
instances where power is exercised by some groups at the expense of
others, and where the exercise of power thus generates conflict: the
political régimes of Greece and South Africa, to select two of many
possibilities, are clearly not instances where power is conferred on the
régime and exercised by the régime to achieve generally shared social
goals, but rather instances where the exercise of power suppresses the
interests of large but relatively powerless social groups, and generates
conflict. Such cases, it might seem, would indicate the superiority of a

'conflict' conception of power over a 'consensus' one. This would, however, be a most naïve, and, in the end, quite false conclusion. The 'consensus' view of power allows that power may be usurped, and be exercised by some groups to suppress others, but that such an exercise of power represents an imbalance, characteristic of instability of the social system. The exercise of power in such a way may not be an uncommon feature of societies, but as such it is inherently unstable, and not a central feature of the social order. In the consensus view, it is power as a resource for the co-ordination of activities and direction of them to social goals that is an essential feature of the social order, and it is this sort of power that is derived from the normative order. The debate between 'conflict' and 'consensus' theory is therefore not a question of whether societies are characterised by conflict or consensus, conflict between interest groups or the sharing of social norms. All sociologists recognise both as general features of social relations. The debate is not about alternative descriptions of societies, but about the selection of organising principles in the construction of a theory of social order. In the consensus view, the normative order is the central organising principle, and power, in so far as it contributes to social order, is a derivative of this. Whereas in the conflict view, it is power that is the central organising principle, and the normative order that is a derivative of the power structure. The two conceptions are thus in many respects opposites, though this does not mean that they encompass the whole sociological debate concerning the nature of power in society.

The Marxist conception of power, as noted above, treats power as a derivative of productive activities. A concise statement of this view is to be found in Marx's *Preface to the Critique of Political Economy*:

> In the social production of their life, men enter into definite relations that are indispensable and independent of their will, relations of production which correspond to a definite stage of development of their material productive forces. The sum total of these relations of production constitutes the economic structure of society, the real foundation, on which rises a legal and political superstructure and to which correspond definite forms of social consciousness. The mode of production of material life conditions the social, political and intellectual life process in general.[9]

For Marx, it is the relations of production that are the basic features of the organisation of social relations, and from these relations of production that the power structure and the normative order is derived. This view is sometimes regarded as a form of economic determinism, whereby social, cultural and political life is treated as a derivative of and dependent upon the economic base of society. Marx certainly regarded the social, cultural and political life of capitalist society as dominated by the capitalist mode of production. This is not the place for a discussion of conflicting interpretations of Marx's work, but the case can be made here that to view power, and other aspects of the structure of society, as derivatives of the relations of men in productive activities is something quite different from the idea of social relations being determined by the workings of an economic system. First of all, productive relations are themselves social relations. The notion of the capitalist mode of production described the relationship between the worker and his employer, his tools, his fellow workers, and his activities. Labour and productive activities, as noted in the discussion of alienation above (p. 109), do not refer merely to the production of commodities for economic exchange, but to man's productive and creative activities in general. It is thus the social relations between men in their productive and creative activities which represent the basic foundation for the cultural and political aspects of social life. In this view, social inequality and the unequal distribution of power in society follow from divisions in productive activities, or the division of labour. It is the division of labour that gives rise to the unequal distribution of labour and its products, and thus also to the ownership of property.[10] In capitalist society, the distinctive feature of the division of labour is the division between labour and capital, between wage labourers and the owners of property. Property, which is one aspect of the division of labour, is the basis of power relations. Marx thus sees the state, the institutions of political power in society, as representing and reflecting the interests of the dominant class in the relations of production.

> The executive of the modern State is but a committee for managing the common affairs of the whole bourgeoisie.[11]

In Marxist terms, then, power is a derivative of the social relations of production.

With the three theories of the nature of power in society outlined, attention may be drawn to a further distinction concerning the nature of power in society. In both the Marxist and what we have termed 'conflict' conceptions of power, increases in power in some sectors of society are always met by decreases in others. Power is always exercised by some groups at the expense of others. Power thus appears as some sort of fixed quantity, the possession of power always being matched by subjection to power. However, in the 'consensus' view of power, where it is seen as a resource for achieving social goals, it is not such a fixed quantity, but may be generated or eroded. This is because the exercise of power by those on whom it is conferred does not imply a corresponding lack of power on the part of those who confer it. Thus, it may be argued that a democratic government that carries the confidence of its population may be a powerful one, in that it is able to carry through its programme, but that where such a government has lost the confidence of its people, it will be weak and ineffective. Peter Blau has suggested that if the exercise of power is seen to be unfair, various processes will tend to erode it: people subject to it may feel that they have little to lose by opposing it, and, furthermore, in the course of their opposition they may develop an ideology of opposition which will give them further strength in their challenge. On the other hand, individuals or groups in positions of power may achieve various benefits by the co-ordination of the activities of those subject to their power, and by passing on some of these benefits, their power may be enhanced.[12] Thus, if a local government increases its efficiency in providing local services, its popularity, and hence power, may increase. In the end, however, it could be argued that increments of power can occur only through the reduction in strength of opposition to power: even if popular confidence would seem to increase the power of a democratic government without depriving other groups of power, such increase of power does in fact mean an increase in ability to overcome opposition. If power is conceived as a social relation, rather than some impersonal, and perhaps rather mystical, 'force' of the social system, then it would seem that the notion of power as a resource must be rejected. As a social relation, power necessarily implies the power of some individuals or groups *over* others. A further problem with the conception of power as a resource is its tendency to confuse power and authority.

AUTHORITY AND IDEOLOGY

Authority, following Max Weber, is usually defined by sociologists as legitimate power. Thus power becomes authority where its exercise is seen as legitimate, right and proper by those who are subject to it. If a policeman secures obedience because he is holding either a truncheon or a gun, then he is merely exercising power, but if he secures obedience because people accept that in certain matters it is right that they should obey the instructions of policemen, then he is exercising authority. It might be thought that authority is the exercise of power in accordance with the normative order, but while this may often be the case, it is not always so, because what is in accordance with the normative order is not always what people accept as right or legitimate: as pointed out earlier in this book (p. 78), norms are not the same as opinions. Thus, people may think it right to obey the religious prophet, even though his instructions are contrary to social norms. Alternatively, power which is exercised in accordance with social norms is not always seen as right. Thus, marchers on a demonstration whose path is blocked by policemen may well be stopped only by force. The police may be exercising their power in accordance with social norms, but as it is not accepted as right, as authority, by the marchers, it can only be sustained by force. Max Weber has produced a typology which classifies authority according to its basis of legitimacy. Weber distinguishes three basic types of authority, namely traditional authority, legal–rational authority and charismatic authority.[13] Traditional authority is the exercise of power which is legitimate because it is in accordance with traditions. One type of traditional authority is patrimonialism, a form of administration in which the state becomes the extension of the personal household of the ruler:

> . . . the Pharaoh, who organised armies of slaves or coloni, put his clients in command of them, and clothed, fed and equipped them from his own storehouses, was acting as a patrimonial chief in full personal control of the means of administration.[14]

Patrimonial authority is characteristic of the centralised despotic state. Feudalism represents another form of traditional authority. Here, relations between vassals and ruler are contractual, and associated with a code of honour, whereas in the patrimonial state relations are in the form of personal servitude to the master. Legal rational authority is the exercise of power which is legitimate because it is in accordance with the law, or with written rules. This is the form of authority that is characteristic of the modern state. Governments hold office because they are constituted and elected in accordance with the law. Authority is exercised by bureaucratic officials in so far as they act in accordance with bureaucratic rules. Charismatic authority is the antithesis of both legal rational and traditional authority, and is based purely on the personal charisma, the personal magnetism and exceptional personal qualities of the holder. As such, it may disregard both rules and traditions. The charismatic leader obtains obedience from his followers through their belief in his personal charisma. In its original, theological sense, charisma refers to the spiritual endowment of the individual with grace. In its sociological sense, as used by Weber, it refers to the recognition by others of exceptional qualities in an individual to the extent that they will obey his commands. The leader's charisma lasts only so long as it is recognised by his followers, and if they desert him, then his charisma is gone. The sociological conception of charisma does not refer to inherent spiritual or other qualities, but only to beliefs about such qualities. It is not to be equated, either, with the increasing popular usage of the term, more so in America than Britain, whereby charisma becomes a term for attractive personality. In its sociological sense, the holder of charisma is the religious prophet, the leader of a social movement, the heroic general whose soldiers will follow him anywhere, but not the charming television personality, or the pop singer.

Weber's authority types are what he terms 'ideal' types, which are abstractions, or pure types, and in practice, the exercise of authority may depend on some combination of these types. Thus, in the paternalistic family firm, the authority of the head of the firm may be a mixture of legal rational authority and traditional authority, based partly on the legal contractual obligations of his employees, and partly on their personal loyalty to him as head of the firm. The authority of the political leader may be partly based on the legal rational authority of his office, but also partly on his personal charisma, though, in the case of constitutionally elected political leaders, charisma may be quite rare.

Authority may now be examined in relation to different conceptions of the nature of power. If the exercise of power is seen as primarily derivative of the normative order, as a resource, then, in so far as it is in accord with consensus values, its exercise will be seen as rightful, and hence it will be authority. If, on the other hand, power is seen either as a basic feature of social relations or as a derivative of relations of production, then authority may be seen as the product of attempts by those exercising power to persuade those subject to them that their exercise of power is right and just. Indeed, it is usual for people who exercise power to produce a theory which justifies it, because it is difficult to maintain positions of power if people do not accept them as legitimate. In the sphere of political power, such theories may be termed ruling class, or élite ideologies. For élite theorists, such as the classic Italian sociologist, Vilfredo Pareto, the exercise of power depends partly on the ability of the élite to produce such an ideology whereby it may manipulate the masses.[15] For Pareto, the liberal theory of parliamentary democracy represents one such ideology serving as a guise for élite domination.[16] Pareto, a disillusioned liberal who later became a supporter of Mussolini, was perhaps rather cynical, but the argument that parliamentary democracy does in fact disguise the rule of an élite demands serious attention. It is not unusual to hear members of parliament argue that, because they are democratically elected representatives of the people, they are not answerable for their actions to the members of their party nor indeed, it may seem, to anyone, if as representatives of a particular party they are virtually guaranteed election in a safe seat. The democratic election legitimises the power of the politician. From both the élite and consensus viewpoints, the election confers power on the elected. But whereas for the consensus theorist this power would tend to be exercised for the common good, for the élite theorist it is exercised primarily for the benefit of the élite. For Pareto, the various parties competing for office in parliamentary elections represent not competing élites, but various faces of a single élite – the governing élite.[17]

Piet Thoenes has described various types of élite ideology whereby élites justify their exercise of, or, in the case of would-be élites, their claim to power.[18] Élites of individuals may proclaim themselves to be chosen by revelation: examples of this type would be prophets and certain types of religious groups, though the latter may not be concerned with the exercise of power in this world. Ruling élites may claim that the process of natural selection ensures that power rests in the hands of those best endowed to exercise it. Such a theory, known as Social Darwinism, asserts the biological superiority of the élite, and as such has much affinity with racialist ideologies which assert that the inferior social conditions of a particular racial or ethnic group are a product of their biological inferiority. A more fashionable élite ideology in the modern world is the justification of élite domination in terms of its specific endowments, its excellence in particular branches of activity. The most common variant of this is the justification of the power of the élite in terms of its superior intelligence. It is sometimes believed that an educational system will be fair if it results in the most rewarding and powerful positions in society being given to those who have the highest intelligence, irrespective of their social background. This is sometimes, in the guise of the slogan 'equality of opportunity', dressed up as an egalitarian theory, but is quite plainly an ideology of élite domination. Finally, there is the ideology of the scientific élite, the claim to superiority through the possession of scientific skills. The authority of the 'expert', whose opinion should be accepted not so much because it is based on persuasive arguments, but because he is recognised to be the 'expert' is based on such an élite ideology. The prevalence of this type of ideology is evident where scientific 'experts' establish their authority by the use of an esoteric 'scientific', and hence to the layman largely unintelligible, language. For élite theorists, then, the authority of élites is to be seen in terms of the dissemination of élite ideologies.

With the Marxist conception of power, authority is also to be seen as a product of the dissemination of ideology. But whereas for élite theorists the ability to maintain an ideology may be one of the bases of power, in the Marxist view, both the exercise of power and the control of ideology rest on the productive process. The ideology of the ruling class is dominant because the ruling class controls the productive process.

> The ideas of the ruling class are in every epoch the ruling ideas: i.e. the class, which is the ruling material force of society, is at the same time its ruling intellectual force. The class which has the means of material production at its disposal, has control at the same time over the means of mental production, so that thereby, generally speaking, the ideas of those who lack the means of mental production are subject to it. The ruling ideas are nothing more than the ideal expression of the dominant material relationships, the dominant material relationships grasped as ideas.[19]

In this conception, ruling-class ideologies are not simply justifications of class rule, but dominate a much wider sphere of thought, though such ideologies are always to be seen as reflecting ruling-class interests. Thus the emphasis on offences against property in the criminal law may be seen to reflect the interests of property-owning classes. Religious teaching, too, may be pervaded by ruling-class ideologies, as where the poor are taught that they should be humble, obedient, and contented, and that their rewards will come in the next world, and that the division of the social world into rich and poor is divinely ordained. In the control of the mental means of production, the ruling class is able to exercise control over such institutions as the mass media and education. In the Marxist view, then, authority and indeed the normative order itself are to be seen in terms of ruling-class ideologies.

One final point to be made about authority in society is the need to distinguish it from institutionalised power. Power may be exercised in an institutional, legal framework, but this does not necessarily mean that its exercise will be accepted as legitimate, as right, by those subject to it. If authority implies the acceptance of power as legitimate, then it follows that institutionalised power does not always constitute authority. This is no mere question of definitions. Institutionalised power is power exercised in accordance with the normative order, but, as has been noted earlier, people do not always accept the exercise of power in accordance with social norms as authority. The power of a town council is institutionalised; it is exercised within the institutional and legal framework of local government, yet the extent of its authority depends on how far the citizens of the town regard the exercise of power as rightful. If significant numbers of citizens believe that the council does not in fact represent the people in any way, but is merely a self-serving body, using its power for its own ends, then it might be said that the council has no authority. It may be recognised that the power of the council is exercised legally, and in accordance with constitutional procedures, but the law and constitutional procedures will be seen not as principles which are served but as means to be used toward some ulterior end. Now it should not be thought that institutionalised power lacks authority merely when people disagree with the particular way in which it is exercised. People may think that the policies of the town council are wrong, but still believe that it is right for the council to make the decisions which they think best. Institutionalised power differs from authority where the legitimacy of the institutions and constitutional procedures themselves is challenged. The point of distinguishing institutionalised power from authority is to indicate that institutional power may not be based upon consensus, and that its continued effectiveness may simply reflect the lack of organised opposition. Thus established political parties may sometimes continue to exercise power even though they fail to represent popular interests, simply because parties articulating such interests fail to crystallise. Furthermore, the distinction between institutionalised power and authority serves to highlight the individualistic emphasis of the concept of authority as developed by Weber. It is not 'society' which decides whether the exercise of power is rightful, but the individual subject to power; and as has been seen, his decision may be contrary to social norms.

SOCIAL CLASSES AND ÉLITES

From the above discussion of power and authority, it will be apparent that, in the Marxist view, the exercise of power in society is an aspect of the relationships between social classes. It is the division of labour in productive activities, the social relations of production, that produces both social classes and inequalities of power. Social classes are defined in terms of relations to the means of production, and the class which controls the means of production is the ruling class. Thus in capitalist society, the two major social classes are those of the capitalists, the owners of property who thereby control the means of production, and the proletariat, the propertyless workers. Class relationships are conflict relationships, and it is the conflict between major classes in society that provides the basic motive force in the production of social change. It follows that the structure of society, the power structure and the normative order are all to be seen in terms of the primary phenomenon of the class structure.

While most sociologists do not accept this framework for the analysis of social class in its entirety, most would nevertheless regard the ordering of society into social classes as a major feature of the structure of society. Sometimes, while the distribution of power is seen to coincide with the division of society into social classes, classes may be viewed as not necessarily reflecting economic divisions in society, but rather political divisions, which may or may not be based on economic divisions. Thus Dahrendorf, in a critique of Marx, argues that property is only a special case of class divisions and power relationships. For Dahrendorf class relationships are relationships of institutionalised power or authority.[20]

More frequently, sociologists conceive of power and social class as separate dimensions of inequality, and often distinguish social stratification into elements of economic class and social status. In this view, which follows Max Weber, power, class and status become separate dimensions of inequality. However, to regard class just as one of several dimensions of inequality is to deny the Marxist view that class relations – productive relations in society – are the basis of social order. From the Marxist perspective, to treat class as a form of economic relation distinct from the social relations of status and power is to depict class as an aspect of the rather narrowly, conventionally defined 'economic' sphere of society. Nevertheless, there is much to be said for regarding power, class and status as distinct dimensions of inequality, so long as they are not regarded as independent. The relationships between these three dimensions may turn out to be very complex, rather than one dimension simply being a determinant of the others.

If power and class, based on productive relations, are treated as separate dimensions, the question of the extent to which the exercise of political power reflects the interests of a particular social class becomes one which has to be investigated empirically in the real world, rather than one to be answered by *a priori* theorising. The Marxist view is sometimes wrongly taken to imply that political power is some sort of mechanical reflection of particular class interests. It is true that Marx regarded the state, the institutions of political power, as primarily an instrument of class rule, and that this view is echoed by Lenin.[21] Domhoff, in a contemporary Marxist analysis of the power structure of the United States, concludes that political power rests primarily in the hands of a power élite, which represents the interests of the American upper class.[22] Miliband, in a comparable study of Britain, concludes that the state élite serves the interest of a ruling class.[23] However, Marx himself indicates in one passage that the state, the institutions of political power, may become some sort of independent, parasitic set of institutions.

> This executive power with its enormous bureaucratic and military organisation, with its ingenious state machinery, embracing wide strata, with a host of officials numbering half a million, besides an army of another half million, this appalling parasitic body, which enmeshes the body of French society like a net and chokes all its pores, sprang up in the days of absolute monarchy. . . .
>
> Under the Restoration, under Louis Philippe, under the parliamentary republic, it was the instrument of the ruling class, however much it strove for power of its own.
>
> Only under the second Bonaparte does the state seem to have made itself completely independent. As against civil society, the state machine has consolidated its position. . . .[24]

It should be admitted that following this analysis, Marx goes on to suggest that the Bonapartist state represents the peasants as a class in French society. The general point to be made here, though, is that the translation of social class interests into political power is to be seen as a process of social action. Thus, it may be that the interests of a class fail to be organised politically, and that therefore such interests never become translated into political power. Conversely, the exercise of political power may, in its institutional form, become divorced from and thus independent of any particular class interests. To illustrate this point we can refer to a comparative and historical study of political parties in Europe and America, undertaken by S. M. Lipset and S. Rokkan, which sets out to examine the factors whereby social cleavages become translated into political divisions.[25] Among their conclusions, the authors suggest that political party divisions of the 1960s are to be seen as a product not of contemporary social divisions, but those of the 1920s. The parties are seen as ossified, excluding new alternatives in politics, and not representing rising contemporary interests. Student protest movements and community action organisations may be seen as forms of organisation of interest which established political parties fail to cater for. What is indicated by this sort of analysis is that while institutional power may develop on the basis of social class divisions, once institutionalised its exercise may be maintained largely because of its institutionalisation: the institutions of political power, the state, become themselves the basis of political power. An extreme, though not uncommon, instance of this situation is the seizure of power through the military coup. The military, developed as an instrument of the state, becomes the master of the state, and whatever other objectives military régimes may hold, a primary one is usually the supremacy of the military. The power of the state is then exercised primarily for the benefit of one executive branch of the state. Military régimes may, however, still represent the interests of a particular social class. A less extreme instance is where established political parties continue to exercise power largely because they are established, even though they have lost the sort of support on the basis of which they rose to power. It is thus possible to see the notions of the rule of governing élites as on the one hand based on social-class interests and on the other hand independent of class interests but based rather on techniques of maintaining power as in some degree complementary.

For Marx, the two major classes in capitalist society are the capitalists, the owners of the means of production, and the proletariat, propertyless wage workers. In modern Britain most sociologists would regard a rather different division, the division between the working class and the middle class, corresponding broadly to the families of manual and non-manual workers respectively, as the major class division. The average incomes of non-manual workers are substantially higher than those of manual workers. Conditions of work are far better, and security of employment far higher for non-manual workers in comparison with manual workers. A far higher proportion of non-manual than manual workers participate in occupational pension schemes, and non-manual workers are much better paid in times of sickness. Outside the immediate occupational sphere, middle-class families are relatively immune from criminal prosecution. The educational opportunities for middle-class children are far superior to those of working-class children, partly because middle-class families live in middle-class areas which enjoy superior educational provision, and also partly because of the emphasis on middle-class values in schools and colleges. Partly because of their higher incomes, but also because of their greater security of employment and favour with financial institutions, middle-class people are much more able to buy the better houses enjoying the better environments, and to gain generous tax concessions on mortgage repayments in the process. The political parties and political institutions, as are the educational, legal and other social institutions, are dominated by the middle class.

The division between the working class and the middle class on the basis of whether occupations are manual or non-manual is very crude, and does not take into account the complexities of the contemporary class structure. It is, perhaps, dubious to regard routine non-manual workers such as clerical workers as middle class: not only are their economic rewards no greater than those of skilled manual workers: their numbers also include a significant proportion of the very lowest paid workers in Britain.

Taking occupation as the basis of the class structure, occupations may be classified according to a hierarchy of reward, and where this is done, usually five or six classes are distinguished. Following Parkin,[26] the following occupational categories might be ranked hierarchically to indicate the rough distribution of reward in modern industrial society:

Professional, managerial, and administrative
Semi-professional and lower administrative
Routine white-collar
Skilled manual
Unskilled manual

These categories approximate the classifications used by the Registrar-

General for the Census and other official statistics, and by market research organisations. They are often useful for classifying the population for purposes of empirical research. It may, for example, be useful to compare the incidence of children receiving higher education, or perhaps the incidence of children appearing before magistrates' courts on the basis of such an occupational classification of their parents. The knowledge gained from such studies provides a basis for the understanding of the workings of the class structure in society, but it would be a mistake to regard social classes as classifications invented by sociologists and social survey researchers to help them interpret their findings. Social classes, in the last analysis, only exist in that they are recognised to exist. The social order is dependent upon people's definition of the social order. Discrimination against people of lower social classes occurs because they are recognised to be of lower social classes. The distinction that is sometimes made between 'objective' classes, as defined by sociologists, and 'subjective' classes, as recognised by people in society, is therefore erroneous. It is true that sociologists' theories of social class are considerably more complex and elaborated than everyday conceptions of class, but these theories must be based on distinctions that are socially recognised, and everyday conceptions of social class are based on the recognition of class in the structure of society.

Social classes, then, are not mere social categories, descriptive layers of a hierarchy of inequality, but are recognised social groups, possessing distinct interests, and adhering to distinct sets of values and ideologies. Thus, the development of urban motorways serves the interests of people who live in out-of-town suburbs and will use the motorways for commuting by car, in other words, predominantly middle-class people. On the other hand, they are detrimental to the interests of people whose homes are displaced by or adjacent to the motorway, and do not own motor-cars, predominantly working-class people. Urban motorways tend to be built through working-class rather than middle-class districts because the acquisition of land through compulsory orders is cheaper in working-class districts. Middle-class values emphasise achievement, career aspirations and ambition, drive, independence, good manners and politeness. Working-class values emphasise solidarity, collectivism, homeliness, neighbourliness, sociability and not 'putting on airs and graces'. In any society, the ideology of the dominant class tends to prevail. 'Queen and country' and 'free enterprise' are embedded in middle-class ideology in contemporary Britain.

In the analysis of social stratification, sociologists, following Max Weber, frequently distinguish between social class and social status. In this distinction, class refers to the individual's opportunities for economic rewards, whereas status refers to his social estimation of honour and prestige. Max Weber saw social status as independent of social class, and it is, indeed, not too difficult to find examples of people in modern society whose class and status positions would seem to be incongruous. The successful bookmaker may rank low in social status, though he may rank high in his economic rewards. The clergyman may enjoy fairly high social status, if not so high as half a century ago, but ranks quite low in the receipt of economic rewards. Yet while it may be possible to think of many similar examples, it is much more generally the case that social status and prestige tend to coincide with economic and material rewards. In general, the lowest paid occupations in society enjoy the lowest social status and prestige, and the highest paid the highest status and prestige. There is a sociological theory which argues that it is necessary for the functionally most important positions in society to receive the highest economic rewards, prestige and social status in order to ensure that they will be filled by the best qualified people, and to ensure that people will be sufficiently motivated to undergo the long periods of training often required for such positions.[27] There are many objections to such a theory which cannot be dealt with here, but it may be asked why material rewards of class and symbolic rewards of status should coincide. If social stratification is required to ensure that the best people fill the most important positions, why should it not be sufficient to provide either high social status or high economic rewards rather than both together? For an explanation of the close relationship between class and social status, it is useful to return to the Marxian view of productive relations as the basis of the class structure. The dominant class in the productive system is also in a dominant position in terms of its influence on values of social honour and prestige. The dominant positions in society thus tend to carry the highest social status and prestige because those who hold these positions exert a dominant influence on the values of social status and prestige. The social status hierarchy of a society may thus represent an aspect of the ideology of the dominant class, and may in fact be challenged by subordinate classes. Thus the English public school accent in middle-class circles indicates that its bearer is 'well spoken' and confers high social status, whereas in working-class circles it may be regarded as 'talking posh' and a subject for ridicule. Returning to the notion that the most important positions in society receive the highest material and symbolic rewards, it is not really very easy to see just which are the most important positions. On the face of it, sewage workers and refuse collectors would seem to be of greater functional importance than accountants and solicitors, though conventionally the latter groups are regarded as the more important people. Just as the dominant class is in a position to influence the values of social honour and prestige, so it is able to influence the socially held conceptions of which occupations are most important. Thus, the most important positions in society are usually those held by members of the dominant social class. 'Importance' is really one facet of social status and prestige.

If we regard social status as primarily a derivative of social class, it might seem to be rather superfluous to distinguish between class and status. The distinction remains important, however, for two major reasons. First of all, to say that social status is primarily a derivative of social class does not mean to say that social status is a mechanical reflection of social class any more than the view of power as a derivative of productive relations implies that the exercise of political power is a mechanical reflection of the class structure. Evaluations of social status and prestige develop through the processes of social relations of class in such a way that there may well be considerable discrepancies between people's class and status position. Status evaluations may change less rapidly than the economic rewards of particular positions. Thus, the social status of clergymen has declined relatively little in comparison with the sharper decline of their relative economic position. New forms of obtaining lucrative economic rewards may be regarded as less honorific than traditional forms. Thus, in nineteenth-century England, rent from land was more honorific than profits from manufacture. Certain qualifications for high social status cannot be acquired solely by economic means. Thus, the successful businessman cannot acquire for himself a public school education, though he may be able to acquire it for his children. If he is the genuine self-made man, even wealth may be insufficient to acquire places for his children at one of the more famous of the élite public schools. Thus, Harrow requires all applicants for places to be sponsored by an old boy of the school. Wealth tends to become honorific the further its holder is removed by generation from its original accumulation.

The second major value of the distinction between social class and social status is that it serves to clarify some of the complexities of the class structure. One of the problems of distinguishing the working class from the middle class is that this distinction itself sometimes turns out to be one of status rather than class. Thus, the clerical worker may be distinguished from the manual worker not on the basis of economic rewards, but rather on the basis of his assertion of middle-class *status*, adherence to middle-class values, and the attempt to adopt a middle-class style of life. Some of the finer distinctions of social class may also turn out to be really distinctions of status. Thus, the distinction within the middle class between upper-middle and lower-middle class, and within the working class between 'roughs' and 'respectable' may turn out to be distinctions not so much in terms of differentials in economic and material rewards, but rather distinctions based on styles of life, patterns of behaviour and consumption. Thus, in working-class districts, the 'respectables' are people who keep themselves to themselves, and are concerned with maintaining appearances, whereas the 'roughs' are more open in their behaviour patterns, and are likely to have closer relations with neighbours.

Class consciousness is sometimes regarded as relatively distinct from basic class divisions, the subjective element of class as opposed to the 'objective' measurement of class. The faults of such a distinction have been noted above (p. 149). Class necessarily entails the social recognition of classes, and thus entails some form of class consciousness, though it is possible to distinguish degrees of class consciousness. In Marxian terms, fully developed class consciousness involves not only the recognition of class divisions, but also the awareness of class interests and how these conflict with the interests of other social classes. Butler and Stokes, in a recent detailed study of British voting behaviour, distinguish between those who see politics in terms of the simple representation of different classes, and those who see politics in terms of class conflict. People who saw politics in terms of the simple representation of classes regarded the Labour Party as the party of the working class, but expressed only rather general views on the Conservative Party:

'No, I tell you I'm not interested in them.'
'They promise all sorts of things; but they don't carry them out.'
'They seem to go back on what they say sometimes.'[28]

People who saw politics in terms of class conflict not only saw the Labour Party as representing the working class, but also saw the

Conservative Party as representing opposing class interests. Among comments on the Conservative Party were the following:

'I don't like them at all; they are more for the money people than the working class.'

'Well, I think when they are in power and there is any Budget it is usually the better class people who come off the best; like income tax benefits.'

'They are not good to the workers. They would squash you down if they could; would have you work for nothing if they could.'[29]

Butler and Stokes found middle-class voters much less likely to see politics in terms of social class, and it is generally the case that less class consciousness is found among middle-class than among working-class people. The main reason for this would seem to be that middle-class people often do not perceive the inequalities of the class system because they rarely suffer from the discrimination and deprivation which it entails. Apart from economic inequalities, middle-class people are usually treated with more respect and consideration by public officials and others in positions of power than are working-class people. There is, for example, some considerable difference between the treatment received by the unemployed unskilled manual worker, whose benefits are liable to be stopped if he has not found another job within four weeks, and that received by the unemployed middle-class person who is placed on the professional register. Working-class people may even, on occasion, be turned away from expensive hotels on account of their accent and dress.

It is true that significant numbers of intellectual socialists have been drawn from the middle class, including several noted leaders. In Britain, about one-fifth of middle-class voters are Labour voters, but while it is sometimes assumed that this fifth vote is based on idealism and beliefs in social equality, there is no real evidence that this is so: if many working-class conservatives think they will be better off under a Conservative government, perhaps some middle-class Labour voters believe that they would be better off under a Labour government. A letter to *The Guardian*, complaining of the high interest rates on mortgages, provides an illustration:

I have no other commitments besides my mortgage, but I am rapidly approaching the status of middle-class bankrupt. I shall fight for Labour in the next election with a motivation born of desperation.[30]

Unfortunately, while much research has been done on working-class conservatism, sociologists have paid little attention to the middle-class Labour voter.

The distinction between class and status serves to clarify some aspects of class consciousness by enabling us to distinguish between class consciousness and status awareness. Thus it may be said that people who are concerned to make fine distinctions between their social inferiors and social superiors, as the inhabitants of Grey Street consider themselves to be definitely superior to those of Black Street, though not quite on a par with those of White Street, or as the 'respectables' distinguish themselves from the 'roughs', are characterised by status awareness rather than class consciousness. Status awareness implies an awareness of the social status order, and the place of oneself and others within it, but does not necessarily involve any conception of the existence of different class interests.

Following the Marxian tradition, the notion of class consciousness may be contrasted with that of false consciousness. An individual is class conscious when he is aware of his class interests, but acquires false consciousness when he has a mistaken view of his class interest. The obvious example is the working-class Conservative voter, though this example is problematic, because it is arguable that in Britain today working-class people are equally mistaken if they believe that the Labour Party genuinely serves the interests of the working class. A less ambiguous example might be the relatively low-paid office worker, who, because he uses the 'staff' entrance and not the 'works' entrance of his firm, and for other, similar reasons, identifies himself with the interests of management rather than with those of the workers of the firm, whereas it might be said that his productive relation with the firm is basically the same as that of the wage worker.

One basic problem in employing the notion of false consciousness is the implication that the sociologist is able to perceive people's objective class interests and to contrast these with people's subjective view of their interests which may be false. As has been noted above, it is mistaken to make a sharp distinction between 'objective' and 'subjective' notions of social class. Social reality is dependent upon people's definition of social reality. If we accept this view, how can the sociologist label certain sets of beliefs concerning people's interests as false? First of all, as I have argued in Chapter 3 (p. 62), it must be allowed that people may be mistaken in their definitions of the situation, through lack of relevant information or through acceptance of false information.

Class interests may be represented by ideologies, and the dominant class – in exercising a dominant influence over the means of communication and persuasion – may be able to persuade members of other classes to accept their ideology, thus giving rise to false consciousness. Thus, working-class people may accept political decision-making as something that is 'not for the likes of us', but is properly the preserve of the members of an élite.

A further problem that is met in utilising the notion of false consciousness is that of defining people's interests, because it is not really possible to distinguish people's 'objective' interests from the values and beliefs that they hold. It might be said that it is in the worker's interests to maximise the proportion of the earnings of his employer that is devoted to wages, but this involves the priority of the value of maximising economic rewards, and the subordination of other values – including, perhaps, those of maximising the worker's influence in the process of decision-making in the organisation in which he is employed. Efficiency, measured by the gross ratio of earnings in relation to costs, may not be compatible with the values of democratic organisation. If interests are not altogether separable from people's values and beliefs, then it becomes difficult to assert that a particular set of values and beliefs is contrary to a person's interests and therefore indicative of false consciousness. One approach to the problem is to regard a person's objective interests as those which he has by virtue of his social role. Thus, Dahrendorf argues that just as role expectations are derived from the structure of society and confront the individual as such, so role interests may also be seen as derived from the structure of society.[31] This is a useful notion in that it links the definition of people's interests to their social relations, but does involve treating roles deterministically as external to the individual and rather as laid out by society for him. The limitations of such a conception of role were discussed in Chapter 5 (pp. 84–5), where it was argued that such a conception must be balanced with the notion of creativity in role playing.

False consciousness may be related to alienation, in so far as alienation may be seen as a cause of false consciousness. If an individual is alienated in his roles from his activities, from his true self, then it might be said that he is unable to perceive his true, 'objective interests', and is thus characterised by false consciousness. For example, the student who sees his educational courses solely as a means to acquire paper qualifications may be regarded as alienated. He may believe that it is in his interests for his studies to be limited to the minimum required for securing the given qualifications, but it might be said that his 'objective' interest as a student is to maximise his knowledge and personal development through this in his studies. Yet in this example it is difficult to separate interests in education from educational values. As has been noted (Ch. 5, p. 109), alienation is itself a value concept, and its association with false consciousness does indicate that the statement that an individual fails to perceive his 'objective' interests may be a value judgement. False consciousness tends to imply that the individual's consciousness of his position ought to be other than it is.

To conclude the discussion of false consciousness, the problems it imposes are such that it should be used by the sociologist with caution, but this does not mean that it should be discarded. Just as people may be misinformed, manipulated or misled so that they arrive at a false definition of the situation, so they may hold a false definition of their class situation and class interests. Some of the problems raised by the notion of false consciousness will be reconsidered in the concluding chapter.

In the above discussion, the concepts of role and class have been linked. It is through the concept of role that the analysis of the class structure can be linked with the sociology of everyday life. In one sense, an individual's social class may be seen as one of his roles and as an aspect of his self-identity. He may perceive that others have expectations of him as a member of a particular social class, and particular social classes may constitute generalised others, or reference groups, to which he orientates his behaviour. He may derive some of his social norms from his class or status group as a reference group, as the middle-class housewife follows the norm of 'keeping up appearances' and the 'ordinary' working-class housewife that of neighbourliness. Alternatively, class and social status roles may be seen to intervene in other roles which the individual plays. The interaction between individuals in the respective roles of social security claimant and social security official is thus influenced by the normally different class positions of the role players. It follows from the discussion in this chapter of the basis of social class (p. 148) that occupational and class roles are closely related.

It has been argued in this chapter that the distribution of power in society, the basis of authority in society and the class structure of society should be seen as closely interrelated. At the same time, the vulgar Marxist conception of the exercise of power and the basis of authority as more or less mechanical reflections of the class structure has been rejected. The development of the institutions concerned primarily with the exercise of power, the institutions of the state, may result in their relative independence from specific class interests. At the same time, dominant class interests may not always succeed in pervading the institutions of political power. The normative order, too, may attain a degree of independence, so that commonly held ideas about what is right, and about what is the legitimate basis for the exercise of power, may not always simply reflect dominant class interests. It is important to see the exercise of power and authority and the class structure of society as relatively independent because the relationship between them depends not upon the impersonal operation of a social system, whether it be capitalist or some other, but upon the social action of individuals, and groups in society. If we consider whether or not the interests of motorists, motor manufacturers, road construction firms and road haulage associations prevail in the development of urban transport planning, it is relevant to note that motoring interests coincide more or less with the economically dominant interests in society. Yet the process of making the decision to develop urban motorways and multi-storey car parks, or alternatively, to develop public transport systems instead, does not follow automatically from the dominance of particular class interests but is largely dependent on the action of individuals and groups whereby group interests are organised and articulated. An urban motorway project may be prevented by well organised and determined opposition. It is true that in such processes of decision-making, middle-class groups are usually able to organise more effectively than working-class groups, and that, overall, the dice is heavily loaded against the interests of **working**-class groups: the influential 'expert' planners and administrators, themselves middle class, associating with middle-class people in their social life and sharing middle-class attitudes and values, are likely to favour middle-class interests. The following passage from a planning textbook written by a top British planner explicitly champions class values.

In a huge city, it is a fairly common observation that the dwellers in a slum area are almost a separate race of people, with different values, aspirations and ways of living . . . one result of slum clearance is that considerable movement of people takes place over long distances, with devastating effect on the social groupings built up over the years. But, one might argue, this is a good thing when we are dealing with civic pride. The task surely is to break such groupings even though the people seem to be satisfied with their miserable environment and seem to enjoy an extrovert social life in their own locality.[32]

Yet ultimately, it is social action, the organised activities of individuals, and not the class structure, that directly determines the course of events.

SOCIAL EQUALITY AND DEMOCRACY

Theories which set out to explain class divisions in society as fundamental features or requirements of social organisation may be used by those who seek ideological justifications for prevailing social inequality. If the division of society into classes is an inevitable, or, in the case of functionalist theory, a necessary feature of society, then, so it may be said, it would be futile, or even perhaps socially harmful, to attempt to remove or alter existing class divisions. Theories which proclaim the inevitability of élite domination in society, and that revolutions only succeed in replacing one élite with another may serve as justifications of the power of an élite. Furthermore, if such theories also proclaim, as did that of Vilfredo Pareto, that the maintenance of élite domination depends on the exercise of manipulation and force, then they may be used to justify the exercise of power based on manipulation or force. Mussolini's Fascist State derived some of its intellectual dressings from the work of Pareto. This is not to suggest that the moral justifications of social inequality and the exercise of power follow logically from the sociological theories that are employed to support them. It is rather the case that when sociological theories proclaim particular features of the organisation of society as universal, such features tend to be viewed as therefore good or at least necessary evils. In fact, the logic of such statements of universal features of social organisation is usually faulty, based on the premise that because certain things have always been so in the past, therefore they will continue to be so in the future. The claim of élite theorists of the inevitability of élite rule is based on historical evidence that all societies have been ruled by élites, coupled with dubious assumptions about 'human nature'.[33]

If the distribution of political power in society is closely related to the class structure and social inequality, then it follows that the pursuit of the ideal of democracy, the equal distribution of power in society, must also involve the pursuit of the ideal of social equality. Whatever formal arrangements may be devised to guarantee political democracy, arrangements such as universal suffrage and parliamentary representation, class divisions will tend to ensure that political power is concentrated and exercised primarily for the benefit of dominant classes. Through their control over resources and because key positions of power in society are usually held by their members, socially and economically dominant classes are able to exercise a dominant influence over political decision-making. Today, much concern is often expressed in the press over the problems of impoverished and deprived communities within British cities. Suggestions are made as to the way local authorities, welfare agencies and other government bodies might cope with the problems of these areas. Somewhat less attention is paid to the powerlessness of such deprived and impoverished communities and their inability to influence the actions of political authorities. If economically disadvantaged groups were able to gain political power through democratic processes of elections and parliamentary representation, then such power would surely be used to rectify such disadvantages and to create greater social and economic equality, by such measures as the redistribution of wealth through changes in taxation and welfare benefits. In Britain, Labour governments have consistently failed to reduce social inequality.[34] Some commentators have suggested that this is because they have not tried, but have put other priorities first. Alternatively, it may be argued that the failure of ostensibly socialist governments to erode social inequalities indicates that effective power under socialist parliamentary governments remains in the hands of economically and socially privileged classes.[35]

There are, however, theorists of democracy, who not merely separate questions of political democracy and social equality, but even argue that class divisions in society are actually supportive of democracy.[36] In its essentials, the argument is that democracy depends upon competitions between political parties, and that the best basis for such competition is party divisions based on class divisions. According to one argument, class parties are integrative and unifying, whereas parties based on religious or regional divisions may be more divisive.[37] This may be so: a comparison of party divisions in Northern Ireland and England would support such a conclusion. It could also be argued that the British Labour Party has done much to integrate the working class into the political system. Yet the argument that party divisions based on class divisions support democracy is in reality the argument that such divisions ensure the stability of parliamentary democracy and the preservation of the *status quo*. Democracy is equated with the prevailing political system, and the question of political equality, save in formal terms, is neglected. If the class basis of political divisions appears to be in danger of erosion, the problem is not, in this view, that certain social classes might not be represented, but rather that 'extremist' groups might rise up and threaten the institutions of parliamentary democracy. The question of whether parties actually represent the interests of the classes who support them is anyway rarely asked, because it is usually assumed that if a party gains its support from a particular social class, then it automatically represents the interests of that class. Yet it is at least questionable whether the British Labour Party in office has consistently represented working-class interests.

Parliamentary democracy based on competing parties drawing their support from different social classes is a political system of competition between élites, and the democratic values that such a system maintains may turn out to be the values of these élites, which are defended against those of the masses. It is arguable that such a system of competition prevents the domination of a single élite, but on the other hand the case can be made that such competition is more apparent than real, and that in effect the competing élites comprise the diverse faces of a single, more or less unified élite. It might be said that senior British parliamentarians of the Conservative and Labour parties have common interests which outweigh their party differences, and much the same could be said for politicians in local government.

For those who believe in appeals to the beneficence of élites for the solutions of problems of deprived and impoverished communities, it is one of the sad lessons of sociology that élites tend to serve their own interests. This may appear unduly cynical, and is not to suggest that élite members may not act from humanitarian and altruistic motives. They will, however, conceptualise social problems in terms of their own definitions of the situation, in terms of their own view of the social world, and if they are predominantly drawn from a particular social class, their view of the social world will be the view of that particular class.

7. Objectivity, Values and Social Action

The perspectives of sociology set out in the first chapter of this book provided the basis for the elaboration of a wide, though far from exhaustive, range of sociological concepts in subsequent chapters. I endeavoured to indicate in that first chapter how the four chosen perspectives might complement one another, and throughout the book have tried to indicate the connexions between the different concepts discussed. Yet while it has been possible to show systematic relationships between some of the concepts considered, as, for example, between definition of the situation, reference group and role, on other occasions comparisons between concepts have also revealed contradictory propositions. It is the purpose of this chapter to highlight the problem of these contradictions, and to indicate how they can be accommodated. The discussion requires a consideration of some of the fundamental methodological problems of sociology, which will lead, in conclusion, to an assessment of the role of the sociologist in relation to social and political action.

OBJECTIVITY
The most serious problems to be faced relate to the question of objectivity in sociology. Put simply, some of the concepts discussed, notably that of the definition of the situation, involve the proposition that there can be only alternative subjective constructions of social reality, and that there can be no independent 'objective' viewpoint; whereas others, notably false consciousness, imply that the sociologist can judge people's subjective assessments of their situation to be false from an objective standpoint.

When it is said that there are only alternative subjective experiences of social reality, what is meant is that it is not possible to give an account of social phenomena which is independent of the subjective interpretation of the observer. Any interpretation of social reality will depend upon the perspective, the set of concepts, the very language employed by the observer. This book began with the proposition that

161

sociology should be defined in terms of its *perspective* on social reality: the sociologist's interpretation of social reality is the subjective interpretation of the sociologist, dependent upon the conceptual framework that he takes. If we take, for example, an industrial organisation, we might find that rather different accounts are given of the organisation by management, by the shop steward's committee, and by the sociologist. While the sociologist's account might be more accurate than the other accounts, it would still be dependent upon the particular viewpoint adopted by the sociologist, just as the shop steward's account depends on the viewpoint that the shop steward adopts. This is not any special limitation that is peculiar to the sociologist, for it may be said that *any* account of *any* phenomenon, social or physical, depends upon the frame of reference adopted by the observer. Everyday common-sense knowledge, sociological knowledge, even the knowledge of the natural sciences, are dependent upon conceptual framework adopted for the acquisition of such knowledge. Perspectives are the basis for subjective interpretations of phenomena, but they are not the personal creations of isolated individuals: they are produced socially through social interaction. Common-sense perspectives of everyday life derive from the social interaction of everyday life, and are learned and modified in the course of everyday life. The perspectives of science develop through the interaction of the scientific community, and the perspective of sociology develops and is learned by the sociologist through social communication in the sociological community. Knowledge is thus dependent upon frames of reference which are the product of social interaction: knowledge itself is a social product, dependent upon the social community in which it is produced.

Objectivity is sometimes defined as freedom from social influences.[1] Now if it is accepted that knowledge is a social product, this definition is quite unsound, for it would follow that objective knowledge was something unattainable by men, and that in practice there could be no such thing as objectivity. The definition of objectivity as freedom from social influences implies that knowledge is not created by men, but is there in advance, waiting to be discovered by man. In this view, it would be the task of the sociologist studying the industrial organisation to look for the 'objective' reality behind the appearances. Such a view would neglect the social basis of the development of the sociologist's perspective. Alvin Gouldner has described this conception of objectivity as 'objectivism', and has pointed out how such a view is incompatible with the sociological perspective.

The objectivist thinks that 'objective' truth is that which exists apart from the men who constitute it, and thus existing *apart* from their values, interests, or 'attitudes'. He assumes that truth is that knowledge of the world which would be cleansed of the impurities presumably brought by men's presence: their values, sentiments, attitudes or interests. The objectivist rejects knowledge as a social product, produced by himself as a social being in some social collaboration with others; he tacitly rejects the idea of knowledge as a social product, even if he himself happens to be a sociologist.[2]

The 'objectivist' standpoint, to use Gouldner's term, implies that knowledge as a social product is somehow distorted knowledge, and that escape from social and human influences is needed to remove the distortions. This proposition derives from the confusion of the social character of knowledge with the presence of ideological distortion, prejudice, and bias in accounts of social reality. That knowledge is a social product carries no implications that socially produced knowledge is untrue: if it did, we would be left with the view that truth is unobtainable, for all knowledge would inevitably be distorted by social influences. At the same time, it is possible that the personal and social circumstances of an observer may influence him in such a way that his account is biased, and thus at least partially false. All knowledge is a social product. The sociological perspective employed by the sociologist in his account of an organisation is a social product; whether or not his account is biased or true is quite another question. If he sympathises with either the workers or the management of an industrial organisation to the extent that he ignores evidence which is inconsistent with the view of either of these groups, then it may be said that his account is biased. It is biased not because the account fails to measure up to some independent, already present, 'objective' account, but because the sociologist has allowed his sentiments to interfere with his methods of study. Objectivity in sociology is to be found in the methods of study, not in the results. These methods involve the use of logical argument, deductive reasoning, the presentation of evidence to substantiate propositions, the drawing of conclusions that are consistent with the evidence presented and, perhaps above all, the earnest search by the sociologist for evidence that would prove his theories to be wrong. Furthermore, in the pursuit of objectivity, the sociologist clearly indicates how he has followed such methods, so that the premises and steps of his argument, his assessment of the evidence and the way in which he has gathered it can be subjected to the critical scrutiny of his colleagues. Objectivity requires that the sentiments and personal preferences of the sociologist be subordinated to these methods.

It is not itself a guarantee of truth, for while pursuing these methods the sociologist may make mistakes, or his evidence may be inadequate. Without pursuing objectivity, however, the sociologist cannot hope to arrive at truth.

Some phenomenological sociologists, in their critique of 'objectivist' sociology, have gone so far as to reject objectivity altogether. Thus, Phillipson writes:

> Sociological theories are indexical accounts by sociologists of the social world and, like anybody else's accounts, they are glosses of the experiences which comprise that world. In this sense they carry no special privileged status as being more 'objective' or nearer the 'truth' than the accounts of anyone else.[3]

An account is 'indexical' when its meaning cannot be grasped outside the particular context in which it is used: its meaning can only be understood in the context of the full social and personal circumstances of its utterance; circumstances which will include the personal biography of the person who renders the account and the social situation in which it is presented. To simplify the argument here, 'indexical' accounts may be taken to mean subjective accounts. The point at issue here is that if this argument is true, then there would seem to be no reason why a sociologist's account should be preferable to anyone else's. The only reason, according to Phillipson, is that people might find practical uses for the sociologist's account.[4] Yet according to the phenomenological view, sociological theories are not in any event the sole preserve of the sociologist. As indicated in Chapter 1 (p. 10), every member of society has his own perspective by which he orders social reality, his own common-sense sociological theory. If the sociologist's theory is no more objective than anyone else's, then it would seem to be indistinguishable in status from anyone else's: if there is nothing more to a published treatise on sociological theory than to an impromptu lounge bar opinion, then sociology cannot be treated as a serious academic discipline at all. Ultimately, the denial of objectivity in sociology is the denial of academic sociology itself. What distinguishes the sociological account from the common-sense account is that it is based on the application and presentation of objective methods, and the subordination to these methods of sentiments and other personal preferences. This does not mean that the sociologist's account is *the* 'true' account. He may make mistakes, and even his methods may prove inadequate for the collection of his evidence: but, in so far as he has set out his methods, it will be possible for other sociologists to review them critically, to replicate his studies, and to reassess the evidence for his theories. By such social processes, sociological knowledge advances. The sociological account is not the 'true' account to replace 'false' common-sense theories. It is even possible that the sociologist's account, though produced through the application of objective methods, might, through mistakes and misinterpretations, be untrue, and that a common-sense account of the same phenomenon arrived at intuitively be true. Such an instance would not indicate the superiority of common-sense over sociological methods, any more than would the occasional accuracy of astrological weather forecasts indicate their superiority over meteorological ones. At the same time, it could be a misleading analogy to contrast common-sense and sociological accounts of the social world with mystical and scientific accounts of the physical world, for the perspective of the sociologist is not an alternative to everyday common-sense perspectives, but one that, as I hope to have shown in this book, encompasses and builds upon them.

Some further discussion of the distinction between the inherent social character of knowledge on the one hand and ideological distortion and bias on the other is now called for, as these may be easily confused. Distorted accounts may be the result of personal prejudices, interests and biases, in which case social influences would not seem to be directly involved. Thus, an account may be deliberately distorted and falsified in the interests of those for whom it is prepared, as might occur when an official inquiry into a scandal produces a 'whitewash' report: the 'Dean' report on the Watergate scandal, an official White House report which the author subsequently denied writing, serves as a topical example here. Alternatively, the prejudices of an observer, his ability to maintain beliefs in the face of evidence which clearly shows them to be false, will result in a distorted account even if there is no deliberate deception involved. In both these instances, it might be said that distortion is the result of personal interests and psychological factors, rather than social influences. Social influences lead to distortion when it is the social situation of the individual that leads him to misconstrue evidence, accept statements for which the evidence is clearly inadequate, to disregard logic, and to ignore evidence which fails to fit the desired conclusions. Thus it may be that by virtue of his membership of a particular social class an individual forms a mistaken view of social reality, as in the case of the middle-class person who believes that there are no such things as social classes.

False consciousness represents one consequence of the distortion of an individual's beliefs through his social position. It was noted in Chapter 6 (p. 154) how false consciousness occurred when individuals hold mistaken views of their class interests. The social situation of the lower white-collar worker, involving social contacts with middle-class people, may be regarded as one particularly conducive to false consciousness. Thus Dahrendorf, in an analysis of the social structure of Germany, describes lower white-collar workers as the 'false middle class'.

> Basically, the false middle class consists of the workers of the tertiary industries, that is, those who occupy subordinate positions in the ever growing service industries: the waiter and salesgirl, the conductor and postman, the chauffeur and the gas station attendant. . . . Its incumbents are distinguished from all others, inter alia, by the fact that their work forces them to maintain contact much of the time with other people of diverse social circles; superficially, there may well be less social distance between the false middle class and other social strata than there is between any other two strata. But describing this group as 'middle class' is justifiable in one respect only, namely, its consciousness of self.[5]

In judging people to be falsely conscious, the sociologist is not contrasting people's subjective interpretation of their situation with some independent 'objective' reality: or at least, he should not be. Rather, he observes the falsely conscious individual to misconstrue evidence and accept false information about his situation, to perceive his situation non-rationally. As pointed out in Chapter 3 (p. 62), while the reality of society exists in so far as it is experienced by its members, and depends upon people's definitions of social situations, it must be recognised that definitions of the situation may be mistaken.

The objectivity of sociology, I have argued, lies in its methods, methods which demand that the sociologist should not be influenced by his sentiments or his social situation in such a way that they distort his account of social reality. How can we be sure that the sociologist is free of bias, that the sociologist who is a socialist, for example, does not unthinkingly neglect evidence that might be unpalatable to his political views? There can be no guarantee that any particular sociologist is free from bias, and the best that can be expected is that the social inquirer should be committed to objective study. Yet the objectivity of sociology is not dependent upon the infallibility of any particular sociologist, any more than the objectivity of a natural science depends upon the infallibility of any particular scientist. Sociological knowledge is a social product: through the practice of objective methods, sociological accounts can be subjected to the critical scrutiny of the sociological community, a scrutiny whereby biases and other mistakes may be revealed. What is required is that sociological accounts should be presented in such a way that they can be so scrutinised.

It is sometimes argued that in order to be objective, it is necessary for the sociologist to be detached and free from values, save from those of science and scholarship, in his studies. But there is no inherent reason why commitment to values should be incompatible with objectivity: the commitment of the doctor to the health of his patient does not necessarily impair the objectivity of his diagnosis. The commitment to values only inhibits objectivity if it leads to the disregard of logic, and the misuse of evidence, in short, if it leads to bias.

VALUE COMMITMENT

Sociology has long been beset by controversies about the place of values and it would be far beyond the scope of this book to explore every aspect of this controversy. A discussion of values is necessary here because one of the concepts introduced in this book, alienation, is explicitly a value concept. Whether or not it is appropriate for the sociologist to use such a concept depends upon whether he is entitled to make value judgements in his studies. A student of sociology today may be less concerned with this question than with asking what relevance sociology has to the problems of the world, and what contribution the sociologist might make to social and political change. These questions themselves are inextricable from the question of the value commitment required of the sociologist.

The argument that sociology should be value free in its simplest form treats the sociologist as no different, in respect of his values, from the natural scientist. As a sociologist, he should be concerned solely with the detached and disinterested analysis of the social world; the use to which sociological knowledge is put is not a sociological question any more than is the use to which the discoveries of physics are put a question of physics. This does not mean, so the argument runs, that the sociologist should be indifferent to the plight of his fellow man; it does not debar him from advocating social reform, engaging in political activity, or expressing his views on the way he thinks socio-logical knowledge ought to be applied to social problems. He is as much entitled to do this as anyone else in his role as citizen, but when he acts in such ways, he should be clear that he is acting in his role as citizen, and not in his role as sociologist.[6] One argument in support of this idea of separating the sociologist's role as sociologist from his other roles is that, without such a separation, the sociologist may use sociology as a means for pressing his own personal preferences and values. Max Weber expressed concern, for example, that the sociology teacher should not use the lecture theatre for the advocacy of his political views.[7] If the sociologist wished to proclaim his political views – as Max Weber did – then political meetings were the place for this. Yet while it may be important to affirm that sociology should not be made subservient to a particular political, or indeed religious cause, the argument is insufficient to support the view of sociology as a detached and value-free analysis of social life. In the first place, it can be argued that as the sociologist's activities as a sociologist influence social action, therefore the sociologist has a moral responsibility for his actions as a sociologist. In the second place, it may be shown that the very perspective of the sociologist involves value judgements about the nature of man. Thirdly, the idea that the sociologist should compart-mentalise his roles as sociologist and citizen can be shown to be sociologically unsound. These arguments must be considered in some detail.

It is not too difficult to show that sociology influences social action. In general, it may be said that as social action is influenced by the way people define social situations, then if these definitions of the situation are informed by sociological knowledge, then such knowledge in-fluences social action. Class consciousness, producing political action on the basis of social class divisions, may be heightened by the com-munication of sociological theories indicating the significance of social class in the social structure. Indeed, there are those who believe that classes are only recognised because sociologists have made people aware of them.[8] Theories which point to the inevitability of élite rule may, as suggested above (Ch. 6, p. 158), serve as justifications for the power of élites and weaken the activities of those pursuing democratic ideals, thereby serving to perpetuate élite domination. Theories indicating the social functions of social stratification, also discussed above (Ch. 6, p. 150), may provide justifications for prevailing social inequalities, thereby strengthening those who benefit from these inequalities. The communication and social acceptance of a deterministic role theory, discussed in Chapter 4 (pp. 75–80), has far-reaching implications for social action, for it leads to the view that people cannot be regarded as morally responsible for their actions or appealed to as rational beings, but can be made to adapt and adjust by processes of social conditioning and manipulation.

The moral responsibility of the sociologist may be seen to lie in his act of communicating his theory and research to members of society. Such a moral responsibility is also shared, as Paul Halmos[9] has pointed out by natural scientists, or indeed any academic researcher for their communications. If people do have a moral responsibility for the consequences of their actions, then this applies to the physicist researching on nuclear explosives and the biochemist researching on methods of 'germ' or 'chemical' warfare as much as to the sociologist. Today, increasing numbers of scientists recognise their moral responsibilities. For the scientist, the moral responsibility involved in discovering new methods of killing people is clear, because the human consequences of the technical application of these methods is beyond all doubt. Yet many scientific discoveries do not have such obvious consequences in their application. The consequences of scientific discoveries are generally the social consequences of human actions: thus, many features of the modern city, its physical characteristics and patterns of social movement and interaction within it, may be seen to be a social consequence of the invention of the internal combustion engine and its subsequent incorporation in the motor-car. The inventors of the internal combustion engine could hardly have been expected to anticipate its far-reaching consequences: nor, it might be added, could sociologists of the time. It is, nevertheless, the particular concern of the sociologist to consider the social consequences, unintended or otherwise, of any human activities. It may be possible for medical science to devise methods whereby prospective parents can choose the sex of their offspring: estimation of the consequences of such an innovation depends on sociological evidence concerning the possibilities of one sex being preferred more frequently than the other. A dominant preference for boys, for example, could radically change the relative proportion of the sexes; a possible outcome of this might be a decline in population and far-reaching social changes in the relationships between the sexes. Because the sociologist is concerned with the social consequences of human action, the social consequences of his own activities are, as Dahrendorf has argued, intrinsic to his work as a sociologist,[10] whereas the social consequences of scientific discovery are not intrinsic to the work of the natural scientist. Moral responsibility for the consequences of his actions, however, is something that may be said to face any member of human society.

The argument that the perspective of the sociologist involves value judgements concerning the nature of man can now be considered. In illustrating the influence of sociology upon social action, it has been suggested that a deterministic role theory might influence people to accept the view that people cannot be held to be morally responsible for their actions. In propounding such a theory, the sociologist himself makes a moral judgement: if he sees people as socially determined role players then he cannot, with any logical consistency, at the same time believe in the moral responsibility of the individual. Sociologists who adopt a 'society' or 'social system' perspective of sociology implicitly judge the good of society to be above the good of the individual person: as pointed out in Chapter 1, such perspectives involve anti-individualistic conceptions of man. One of the purposes of that chapter in combining different sociological perspectives was to arrive at a humanistic conception of man. Sociologists whose perspectives depict morality as socially determined in such a way that moral beliefs are regarded as only relative to the society in which they are held themselves make a judgement of value on moral statements. It is perhaps one thing to say that the smoking of cannabis is regarded as a crime only because of historical and social reasons, but rather different to say that it is only because of historical and social reasons that the setting of man-traps to catch poachers or the beating of women by their husbands are regarded as criminal.

Now it may be argued that the sociological perspective employed by the sociologist in his studies is something quite separate from his participation in the social world as a moral person: social systems theorists may thus be liberal individualists. Yet if the sociologist does find such a separation necessary, in making it he tacitly admits that his sociological perspective is inadequate in the real social world that he inhabits as a person. Such a separation also involves the compartmentalisation of the sociologist's roles as sociologist and citizen, the implications of which may now be explained.

The discussion of role playing in Chapter 5 (pp. 94–100) suggested that while people may sometimes attempt to compartmentalise the different roles they play, given role performances will in fact be influenced by the other roles an individual plays. The concept of role distance illustrated how diverse aspects of the individual's self, his other roles, may intrude in a given role performance. The sociologist, as anyone else, may well find his other roles intruding upon his role as sociologist. If the particular roles of the sociologist are examined more closely, compartmentalisation will seem even more problematic. To begin with, it is not only sociologists who hold theories about the organisation of society and the ordering of social life. Everyone understands in some way the procedures of social life in their own society. The very engagement in everyday social life presupposes that the individual has constructed a meaningful social world, that he understands and is able to predict the way people he associates with will behave in given social situations. For most people, such theorising about the ordering of the social world may be neither very explicit, nor particularly conscious: some aspects of the social order will be taken for granted, assumed reflectingly, whereas others will be regarded simply as matters of 'common sense'. Yet such social theorising is a prerequisite of social activity, and those who fail in these endeavours, or whose theories and constructions are quite incompatible with those of their fellows, may well end up as inmates of prisons, mental hospitals and other similar establishments. The sociologist, just as everyone else, must employ theories about social organisation in the course of his everyday life: if his role as a sociologist is to be compartmentalised and isolated from his other roles, then it would seem to follow that while in his sociologist role he will employ one set of social theories, in his ordinary citizen and family roles he will employ quite another sort, the taken-for-granted and common-sense theories of everyday life. Such a divorce would surely amount to an admission by the sociologist that his sociological theories have no relevance for participation in and therefore for the understanding of everyday life. The sociologist who thus compartmentalises his roles in the pursuit of detachment and objectivity will in the end only succeed in detaching his sociology from the reality of the real world.

If it is accepted that the practice of sociology entails value commitments, it would seem to follow that the sociologist needs to be as well versed in ethics and moral and social philosophy as in sociology. T. S. Simey, in a discussion which illuminates this problem, has made the point that whereas value-freedom in sociology is usually interpreted negatively as ethical neutrality, it may in fact be interpreted positively as the freedom of the sociologist to hold his own values and to allow these to guide him in the formulation of his research rather than be subservient to the dominant, official values in his society.[11] Simey points out that Max Weber, who is often cited in support of an ethically neutral and detached sociology, advocated value-freedom as an attack on policy-orientated social scientists who accepted the values of the governmental bureaucracy and devoted their efforts to making it more 'efficient'.[12] If the sociologist is morally responsible for his actions, he is responsible for his choice of values. It is quite inadequate merely to conclude that the sociologist should declare his values, as if it is of no consequence as to what they actually are so long as the sociologist is aware of them and shows it by stating them. If the sociologist takes his moral responsibilities seriously, then it matters a great deal what his value commitments are: his choice of values requires very careful consideration and reflection. The discussion of values was prompted here initially by the question as to whether value concepts, such as alienation, have any place in sociological discourse. It would follow from the above discussion that such concepts, far from being an obstacle to an objective sociology, may help the sociologist to clarify his values in relation to his sociological perspective.

SOCIOLOGY AND SOCIAL ACTION

If the sociologist is morally responsible for the choice of his values, it would follow that if in the course of his research he simply accepts the values of those who sponsor the research, then he abrogates his responsibility. Thus social research undertaken to aid the 'efficiency' of industrial management, to prevent juvenile delinquency, or to provide survey evidence to solve problems posed by social planners, would in each case be based on values which are presented to the sociologist, rather than chosen by him. Now it might seem that if the aims of the research sponsors are worthy, the sociologist is entitled to accept their values and undertake research on such a basis. Careful reflection is, however, unlikely to reveal identity of values between sociologist and sponsor. Social welfare agencies or town planners may well be worthy sponsors of social research, but this does not mean that the sociologist should allow the town planner or the social worker to determine the values of his research framework. As has been argued, values are inherent in the perspective of the sociologist.

If sociology were a disinterested and detached study of the social world, then it might be argued it was irrelevant to consider the purpose to which the research should be put, or the intentions of the sponsors. But sociology is not disinterested or detached, and thus the assertion of value freedom in applied social research in practice may mean the subservience of the research to the values of the sponsor. In such a situation the sociologist either identifies with the values of his sponsor, or else he adopts a position of moral irresponsibility. The issue here is not a question of the moral worth of the research sponsor, but instead one of whether sociology is to become a technology, to be used by those who are able to command its services and are able to pay for it, or whether the sociologist is able to retain his own choice of values and thereby maintain the independence of his sociological perspective.

In contemporary sociological debate, with the increasing description of sociological theories as conservative or radical, it might seem that the basic value question for the sociologist would be whether he was for or against the prevailing social order. Yet nothing could be further from the truth, for in vague acceptance of the prevailing social order or in vague denunciations of 'the present social arrangements' or 'the prevailing capitalist system', or even simply 'the system', the sociologist would allow his values to be determined by dominant social values, in the one case simply accepting them and in the other simply opposing them. Vague acceptance of the social order nearly always appears under the guise of value freedom. Thus functional theories of stratification (discussed earlier on pp. 150–51) in the apparently value-free statement that societies require that the functionally most important positions in society be accompanied by the highest rewards, implicitly accepts the dominant values concerning which positions are most important. A theory that implicitly accepts the values of the prevailing social order would involve implicit acceptance of the dominant value system of any society to which it is applied: such a theory may thus support the dominant values of the United States on the one hand and the Soviet Union on the other. Vague denunciations of the prevailing social order are no different in their moral vacuity. Such denunciations appear implicitly in some studies in the area of the sociology of deviance in which the sociologist proclaims himself, explicitly or implicitly, to be on the 'side' of the deviant and thus presumably against the 'side' of law and order. Deviance is socially defined, and thus the sociologist who is for or against deviance has his values defined by society. Most theorists of deviance recognise this and are wary of blanket condemnation of or support for deviance. Thus, in an introduction to a recent collection of papers, Stanley Cohen writes:

> In some cases there is a clear imperative to reject the officially stated aims of social control, and actively – or by implication – lend support to the deviant group. In other cases we might support official aims such as deterrence but be concerned to define the deviant as a different sort of person from that which he is supposed to be. In yet other cases we might unequivocally accept the aims and conceptions of the control system. Faced with acts including marihuana smoking, violent crime and drunken driving, it is clearly meaningless to ask 'Are you for or against deviance?'[13]

However, in a recent development of deviance theory whereby deviance is seen as a political act, a challenge to the authority of those in entrenched positions of power, an implicit championing of the deviant occurs: the deviant is seen as a liberating agent in a repressive society. Thus writes Paul Walton:

> . . . much deviance – both 'political' and 'non-political' – *must* be viewed as a struggle or reaction to normalized repression, a breaking-through, as it were, of accepted, taken-for-granted, power invested common-sense rules.[14]

Since Walton reveals by his use of the term 'repressive' and by other evaluative descriptions that he is opposed to the prevailing order of Britain and the United States, the following passage leaves us in no doubt as to whose side Walton is on.

> . . . behaviour which in the past was conceived of as deviant is now assuming well defined ideological and organisational contours. The politicization of groups such as drugtakers and homosexuals is only the most obvious manifestation: *any attempt to resist stigmatisation, manipulation in the name of therapy or punishment, is a self-conscious move to change the social order.* . . . political marginals such as the Hippies, the Weathermen, the Situationists, the Black Panthers, are creating new styles of political activity on strategies traditionally considered criminal.[15]   (Italics mine)

Walton is on the side of his 'political deviants', a motley collection of social groups, some of which, such as the Angry Brigade, are extremely small, many of which are committed to the use of extreme forms of violence, but whose most clearly apparent common characteristic is that they all seem to possess, in their unorthodoxy or bizarre nature, a degree of perverse glamour, and are thus fashionable organisations to study. In characterising such a variety of deviance as 'struggles against repression', Walton implicitly condones any values that are contrary to those dominant in society. Radical sociologists have sometimes, and with good reason, revealed the moral irresponsibilities of those sociologists who allow their studies to be subservient to industrial and military interests, but, as the above discussion has shown, it would be quite mistaken to think that moral irresponsibility cannot also be found among radical sociologists.

The view that the sociologist should choose the values involved in his research and not allow anyone else to choose them for him has been considered so far primarily on moral grounds. Yet it may be shown that this is not simply a moral requirement, but a requirement for the objectivity of sociological research. If the social researcher accepts the viewpoint and definition of the research problem as posed by the research sponsor, then he takes for granted part of the social order and excludes it from his analysis: his research is likely to provide no more than an embellishment of the sponsor's view of social reality, rather than an objective sociological analysis. A study of social factors related to efficiency in a bureaucratic organisation, which takes as given the official definition of efficiency and fails to analyse it in relation to the values and interests of the various social groups involved and affected by the bureaucratic organisation, does little more than provide an elaboration of the official account of the activities of the organisation. A study of social factors associated with 'problem' families which takes as given the welfare agency's definition of a problem family without considering it in relation to the values, interests and procedures of the welfare agency, and the values and interests of other groups in society, including those defined as 'problem' families, provides merely an embellishment to the welfare agency view of the social world. A sociology which takes as given official values and definitions of problems in the end takes for granted official definitions of social reality, and is thus no more than an elaboration of common-sense definitions of society. As has been argued earlier in this chapter, an objective sociology does not present an independent alternative to common-sense views of social reality. It is not achieved, however, by a mere representation of common-sense views, but by analysis of these views from the standpoint of the sociologist. Accepted definitions of the situation are the starting point, not the conclusions, of sociological analysis.

Dominant social definitions and constructions of social reality, as was pointed out in Chapter 3 (pp. 63–4), tend to represent the values and interests of the rich and powerful, the 'authorities' in society. In so far as the sociologist refuses to take such conventional and official definitions for granted, but chooses his own standpoint, he is committed to a critical position in relation to prevailing values. Alvin Gouldner has argued that if sociology is to be objective it must resist officially defined social theories that are merely 'authoritative'. His case is that the powerful in society, the élites and the establishment, seek acceptance of and conformity with their basic images of social reality, their common-sense theories.

> Conformity with the basic principle of establishment politics – that is, accepting the image of social reality held by the hegemonic élite or at least one compatible with it – is, however, nothing less than a betrayal of the most fundamental objectives of any sociology. The price paid is the dulling of the sociologist's awareness.[16]

An objective sociology may thus be radical in that it may undermine official images of social reality, images which themselves serve to buttress the power of dominant élites. However, this radical character of sociology derives not from a general commitment to opposition to the prevailing order of any society, but from the pursuit of objective sociological knowledge on the basis of critically chosen values.

What, it may be asked, is the relevance of such a sociology to the solution of social problems and the formulation of social policy? It is simply that only objective sociological studies, carried out from the critical standpoint of the sociologist, will provide the knowledge on the basis of which policies and problems can be evaluated and re-appraised. Research which accepts as given the standpoint of those administering social policy is likely thereby to accept and merely elaborate already chosen solutions to social problems. If the research is sponsored, as is sometimes the case, simply to give the organisation or agency a progressive or scientific image or, to provide ammunition to support decisions that have already been taken, then a narrow technological sociology may serve the interests of the sponsors. Only a critical, objective sociology can assist those who genuinely seek to be guided by sociological knowledge in policy decisions.

The pursuit of objectivity represents the commitment of the sociologist to the values of his profession. There may, however, be occasions when he feels that other values should take precedence. In the course of his work, perhaps in the study of an impoverished and oppressed minority, he may decide that it is more important for him to help those he is studying than to prepare an objective account of them. On other occasions, the sociologist may decide that the pursuit of political goals should take precedence over the values of his profession. If, for example, the democratic institutions of his country are overthrown by a brutal military dictatorship, and many of his friends are imprisoned, he may decide to devote himself entirely to the overthrow of the new régime. If the sociologist makes such a decision, he is in effect deciding to stop being a sociologist, at least for the time being, and instead to devote his energies to what seem to him to be more worth-while pursuits. Such a decision may well be a morally courageous one.

This is not to say that the sociologist cannot be a sociologist and political activist at the same time; nor is it implied that the roles of political activist and sociologist, when played by one person, should be neatly compartmentalised. I have argued that roles cannot be compartmentalised. The values adopted by the sociologist in his sociological studies should be compatible with the values he holds in his other roles. But while roles cannot be compartmentalised, they should, nevertheless, be distinguished. Sociology has many implications for political action and social change, but it is not itself a form of political action.

The increasing prominence of radical sociology in recent years may lead some students to believe that by becoming sociologists they may thus become political activists. Such a belief is a delusion. Radical sociologists are not, by and large, political activists at all, but professional sociologists and sociology teachers of varying degrees of academic success, scholarship and intellectual competence. On the other hand, those who seek a sociology that forsakes the pursuit of objectivity in the interests of a particular political or any other cause, should recognise that it is the particular cause that they seek to serve, and that sociology is not for them.

Notes and References

1. The Perspectives of Sociology

1. Examples of their work are C. Wright Mills, *White Collar* (New York: Oxford University Press, 1951); David Riesman, *The Lonely Crowd* (New York: Doubleday, 1953); and William H. Whyte, *The Organisation Man* (Harmondsworth: Penguin, 1960).

2. Emile Durkheim, *The Rules of Sociological Method* (New York: Free Press, 1964 edition), p. 102.

3. Ibid., p. 103.

4. Ralf Dahrendorf, *Essays in the Theory of Society* (London: Routledge and Kegan Paul, 1968), p. 76.

5. Erving Goffman, *Encounters* (New York: Bobbs-Merrill, 1961), p. 152. Also available in Penguin.

6. Ralf Dahrendorf, op. cit., p. 86.

7. Talcott Parsons, 'The point of view of the author', in Max Black (ed.), *The Social Theories of Talcott Parsons* (New Jersey: Prentice Hall, 1964), p. 338.

8. See, for example, Stanley Cohen (ed.), *Images of Deviance* (Harmondsworth: Penguin, 1971). These and similar theories are discussed in Chapter 5.

9. Richard Hoggart, *The Uses of Literacy* (London: Penguin, 1958), pp. 72–3.

10. See Harold Perkin, *The Origins of Modern English Society 1780–1880* (London: Routledge and Kegan Paul, 1969), Ch. 6.

11. E. P. Thompson, *The Making of the English Working Class* (Harmondsworth: Penguin, 1968), p. 303.

12. See, for example, E. A. Nordlinger, *The Working Class Tories* (London: McGibbon and Kee, 1967), Ch. 6. This study provides evidence that a substantial proportion of working-class Conservatives in Britain believe that Labour Party politicians are not sincere in championing working-class interests, but are out to serve their own ends.

13. E. P. Thompson, op. cit., p. 66.

14. David Berry, 'Party Politics and Community Action', forthcoming.

15. Karl Marx and Frederick Engels, *The German Ideology* (New York: International Publishers, 1963 edition), p. 39.

16. See E. P. Thompson, op. cit., pp. 412–16.

2. The Moral Order of Social Life

1. Theodore Geiger (trans. Robert E. Peck), *On Social Order and Mass Society* (Chicago: University of Chicago Press, 1969), p. 43. My discussion of social norms draws heavily on this work.
2. Ralf Dahrendorf, *Essays in the Theory of Society*, pp. 39–41.
3. Ibid., p. 41.
4. Maureen Cain, 'On the Beat: Interactions and Relations in Rural and Urban Police Forces', in Stanely Cohen (ed.), *Images of Deviance* (Harmondsworth: Penguin, 1971), p. 88.
5. Peter McHugh, *Defining the Situation: the Organisation of Meaning in Social Interaction* (New York: Bobbs Merrill, 1968).
6. Emile Durkheim, *Suicide* (London: Routledge and Kegan Paul, 1952).
7. See Robert K. Merton, *Social Theory and Social Structure* (New York: Free Press, enlarged edition 1968), Chs. VI & VII.

3. Social Definitions and Perspectives

1. Erving Goffman, *Relations in Public* (London: Allen Lane, The Penguin Press, 1971), Ch. 6.
2. Ibid., p. 317.
3. Notably Harold Garfinkel, *Studies in Ethnomethodology* (New Jersey: Prentice-Hall, 1967), and Peter McHugh, *Defining the Situation: the Organisation of Meaning in Social Interaction* (New York: Bobbs Merrill, 1968).
4. Peter McHugh, op. cit., Ch. 3.
5. Ibid., Ch. 6.
6. Robert K. Merton, *Social Theory and Social Structure* (New York: Free Press, enlarged edition 1968), Ch. 13.
7. Ibid., p. 477.
8. C. H. Cooley, *Human Nature and the Social Order* (New York: Scribner's, 1902), p. 84.
9. George Herbert Mead, *Mind, Self and Society* (Chicago: University of Chicago Press, 1934), p. 154.
10. Ibid., p. 155.
11. Tamotsu Shibutani, 'Reference Groups and Social Control', in Arnold M. Rose (ed.), *Human Behaviour and Social Processes* (London: Routledge and Kegan Paul, 1962), p. 132.
12. Ralph Turner, 'Role Taking, Role Standpoint and Reference Group Behaviour', *American Journal of Sociology*, Vol. 61 (1956), p. 328.
13. See, for example, W. G. Runciman, *Relative Deprivation and Social Justice* (London: Routledge and Kegan Paul, 1966), Ch. 2.
14. R. K. Merton, op. cit., p. 287.
15. W. G. Runciman, op. cit., p. 14.

16. Ibid., p. 194.
17. Ken Coates and Richard Silburn, *Poverty: the Forgotten Englishmen* (Harmondsworth: Penguin, 1970), p. 146.
18. R. K. Merton, op. cit., pp. 319–22.
19. S. A. Stouffer, et al., *The American Soldier* (Princeton: Princeton University Press, 1949).
20. Anthony Trollope, *Barchester Towers* (Harmondsworth: Penguin, 1957), p. 326.
21. Ibid., p. 355.

4. Role Playing

1. N. Gross, W. S. Mason, and A. W. McEachern, *Explorations in Role Analysis* (New York: Wiley, 1958), Ch. 4.
2. Talcott Parsons, *The Social System* (London: Routledge and Kegan Paul, 1951), pp. 463–4.
3. Ralf Dahrendorf, *Essays in the Theory of Society* (London: Routledge and Kegan Paul, 1968), p. 49.
4. Op. cit.
5. Op. cit., p. 48.
6. George Herbert Mead, *Mind, Self and Society* (Chicago: University of Chicago Press, 1934), pp. 173–8.
7. Ibid., p. 254.
8. C. H. Cooley, *Human Nature and the Social Order* (New York: Scribner's, 1902).
9. George Herbert Mead, 'Cooley's Contribution to American Social Thought', in G. H. Mead, *On Social Psychology* (Chicago: University of Chicago Press, 1964), p. 300.
10. Erving Goffman, *The Presentation of Self in Everyday Life* (London: Allen Lane, 1969), p. 223.
11. Ralph Turner, 'Role-taking: Process Versus Conformity', in Arnold M. Rose, *Human Behaviour and Social Processes* (London: Routledge and Kegan Paul, 1962).
12. Ibid., p. 23.
13. E. Goffman, op. cit., p. 225.
14. Alvin Gouldner, *The Coming Crisis of Western Sociology* (London: Heinemann, 1971), pp. 378–90.
15. E. Goffman, op. cit., p. 62.
16. Ralf Dahrendorf, op. cit., p. 76.
17. Erik Allardt, et al., 'On the Cumulative Nature of Leisure Activities', *Acta Sociologica*, Vol. 3 (1958), pp. 165–72. Numerous other research studies have echoed the findings of this study.
18. J. Diedrich Snoek, 'Role Strain in Diversified Role Sets', *American Journal of Sociology*, Vol. 71 (1966), pp. 363–72.

19. William F. Whyte, 'Where Workers and Customers Meet', in William H. Whyte (ed.), *Industry and Society* (New York: McGraw Hill, 1946).
20. See Robert K. Merton, *Social Theory and Social Structure* (New York: Free Press, 1968 edition), pp. 425–33. Also N. Gross, W. S. Mason, and A. W. McEachern, op. cit., Chs. 15–17.
21. This point is made by Ralph Turner, op. cit.
22. Peter Berger, *Invitation to Sociology* (Harmondsworth: Penguin, 1966), Chs. 6–8.
23. Erving Goffman, *Encounters* (New York: Bobbs-Merrill, 1961), pp. 107–8.
24. Ibid., p. 106.
25. Ibid., p. 139.
26. Alvin Gouldner, op. cit., p. 380.
27. Erving Goffman, *The Presentation of Self in Everyday Life*, p. 224.
28. Robert E. Park, *Race and Culture* (New York: Free Press, 1950), p. 249.
29. Erving Goffman, *Encounters*, pp. 99–100.

5. Negatives in Social Organisation: Alienation and Deviance

1. Philip Selznick, *The Organisational Weapon* (New York: Rand Corporation, 1952), Ch. 7.
2. A. W. Finifter, 'Dimensions of Political Alienation', *American Political Science Review*, Vol. LXIV, No. 2 (June 1970), pp. 389–406.
3. Robert E. Lane, 'The Politics of Consensus in an Age of Affluence', *American Political Science Review*, Vol. LIX (1965), pp. 874–95.
4. Karl Marx, *Economic and Philosophical Manuscripts of 1844* (ed. Dirk J. Struik) (London: Lawrence and Wishart, 1970), p. 108.
5. Ibid., pp. 111–12.
6. Ibid., pp. 112–13.
7. Erich Fromm, *The Sane Society* (London: Routledge and Kegan Paul, 1956), pp. 110–20.
8. Douglas Holly, *Society, Schools and Humanity* (London: MacGibbon and Kee, 1971), Ch. 5.
9. Ibid., p. 91.
10. Ibid., p. 97.
11. David H. Hargreaves, *Social Relations in a Secondary School* (London: Routledge and Kegan Paul, 1967), pp. 37–44.
12. Peter L. Berger and Thomas Luckmann, *The Social Construction of Reality* (London: Allen Lane, 1967), p. 78.
13. Ibid., p. 106.
14. C. Wright Mills, *White Collar* (New York: Oxford University Press, 1951), p. 184.
15. Erving Goffman, *Stigma: Notes on the Management of Spoiled Identity* (Harmondsworth: Penguin, 1968).

16. From Nathanael West, *Miss Lonelyhearts* (New Directions, 1962), pp. 14–15, quoted in E. Goffman, op. cit., p. 7.

17. Reproduced in E. P. Thompson (ed.), *Warwick University Ltd* (Harmondsworth: Penguin, 1970), p. 123.

18. Op. cit., Ch. 5.

19. Jock Young, *The Drugtakers: the Social Meaning of Drug Use* (London: MacGibbon and Kee, 1971), pp. 195–6.

20. Dennis Chapman, *Sociology and the Stereotype of the Criminal* (London: Tavistock, 1968), p. 56.

21. Aaron V. Cicourel, *The Social Organisation of Juvenile Justice* (New York: Wiley, 1968).

22. Emile Durkheim, *The Division of Labour in Society* (trans. George Simpson) (New York: Free Press, 1947).

23. Op. cit., p. 25.

24. Op. cit., p. 79.

25. Op. cit., p. 79.

26. Op. cit., p. 83.

27. Erving Goffman, *Stigma*, pp. 163–4.

28. Robert K. Merton, *Social Theory and Social Structure* (New York: enlarged edition, 1968), Ch. 6.

29. E. H. Mizruchi, *Success and Opportunity: a Study of Anomie* (New York: Free Press, 1964), Chs. 4–6.

30. For example, see Edward L. McDill and Jeanne Clare Ridley, 'Status, Anomia, Political Alienation and Political Participation', *American Journal of Sociology*, Vol. 68 (1962–3), pp. 203–13.

31. Robert K. Merton, 'Social Problems and Sociological Theory', in R. K. Merton and R. A. Nisbet (eds), *Contemporary Social Problems* (New York: Harcourt, Brace and World, second edition, 1966), pp. 808–11.

32. Op. cit., pp. 195–6.

6. Power and Social Inequality

1. Melvin Seeman, 'On the Meaning of Alienation', *American Sociological Review*, Vol. 24, No. 6 (1959), pp. 783–91.

2. Max Weber, *The Theory of Social and Economic Organisation*, Tr. A. M. Henderson and Talcott Parsons (New York: Free Press, 1947), p. 152.

3. Peter M. Blau, *Exchange and Power in Social Life* (New York: Wiley, 1964), pp. 118–25.

4. See, for example, Robert M. Presthus, *Men at the Top, A Study in Community Power* (New York: Oxford University Press, 1964), Chs. 4 and 5.

5. Arnold M. Rose, *The Power Structure* (New York, Oxford University Press, 1967), pp. 9–15.

6. Ralf Dahrendorf, *Class and Class Conflict in Industrial Society* (London: Routledge and Kegan Paul, 1959), pp. 167–9.

7. Ralf Dahrendorf, *Essays in the Theory of Society* (London: Routledge and Kegan Paul, 1968), p. 139.

8. Important figures include Vilfredo Pareto, Gaetano Mosca and Robert Michels.

9. Karl Marx and Frederick Engels, *Selected Works*, Vol. 1 (Moscow: Foreign Languages Publishing House, 1962), pp. 362–3.

10. Karl Marx and Frederick Engels, *The German Ideology* (New York: International Publishers, 1947), p. 21.

11. Karl Marx and Frederick Engels, *The Communist Manifesto*, in *Selected Works*, Vol. 1 (Moscow: Foreign Languages Publishing House, 1962), p. 36.

12. Peter Blau, op. cit., pp. 227–33.

13. Max Weber, op. cit., p. 328.

14. Max Weber, ibid., p. 350.

15. Vilfredo Pareto, *Sociological Writings*, Selected and introduced by S. E. Finer (London: Pall Mall, 1966), p. 244.

16. Vilfredo Pareto, ibid., p. 268.

17. Vilfredo Pareto, ibid., p. 312.

18. Piet Thoenes, *The Elite in the Welfare State* (London: Faber and Faber, 1966), pp. 56–70.

19. Karl Marx and Frederick Engels, *The German Ideology*, p. 39.

20. Ralf Dahrendorf, *Class and Class Conflict in Industrial Society*, Ch. 1.

21. V. I. Lenin, *The State and Revolution* (Moscow: Foreign Languages Publishing House), Ch. 1.

22. G. W. Domhoff, *Who Rules America?* (New Jersey: Prentice Hall, 1967), Ch. 7.

23. Ralf Miliband, *The State in Capitalist Society* (London: Weidenfeld and Nicolson, 1968), Ch. 3.

24. Karl Marx, *The Eighteenth Brumaire of Louis Bonaparte*, in Karl Marx and Frederick Engels, *Selected Works*, Vol. 1, pp. 332–3.

25. S. M. Lipset and Stein Rokkan, 'Cleavage Structures, Party Systems and Voter Alignments: an Introduction', in Lipset and Rokkan (eds.), *Party Systems and Voter Alignments: Cross-National Perspectives* (New York: Free Press, 1967).

26. Frank Parkin, *Class Inequality and Political Order* (London: MacGibbon and Kee, 1971), p. 19.

27. Kingley Davis and Wilbert E. Moore, 'Some Principles of Stratification', *American Sociological Review*, Vol. 10 (1945), pp. 242–9.

28. David Butler and Donald Stokes, *Political Change in Britain* (Harmondsworth: Penguin, 1972), pp. 114–15.

29. Ibid., pp. 112–13.

30. Letter the the Editor, *The Guardian*, 27 August 1973.

31. Ralf Dahrendorf, *Class and Class Conflict in Industrial Society*, p. 178.
32. Wilfred Burns, *New Towns for Old* (London: Leonard Hill, 1963). Quoted by John A. Palmer in Introduction to Robert Goodman, *After the Planners* (Harmondsworth: Penguin, 1973), pp. 27–8.
33. Human nature is seen as characterised by such features as irrationality, veneration of leaders, authoritarianism. Whether or not evidence can be produced for the existence of such traits there is no basis for assuming that they are part of an inherent human nature rather than cultural and social products, features of human characters in particular societies at particular times.
34. For evidence, see, for example, Peter Townsend and Nicholas Bosanquet (eds.), *Labour and Inequality: Sixteen Fabian Essays* (London: Fabian Society, 1972).
35. See Ralph Miliband, *The State in Capitalist Society*, Ch. 4, and Frank Parkin, *Class, Inequality and Political Order*, Ch. 4.
36. Examples are S. M. Lipset, *Political Man* (London: Heinemann, 1960), Chs. 7 and 8, and Hannah Arendt, *The Origins of Totalitarianism* (London: Allen and Unwin, 1958), p. 315.
37. Robert R. Alford, Party and Society, *Voting Behaviour in Anglo-American Democracies* (London: Murray, 1964), p. 339.

7. Objectivity, Values and Social Action

1. See, for example, Quentin Gibson, *The Logic of Social Enquiry* (London: Routledge and Kegan Paul, 1960), p. 77.
2. Alvin Gouldner, *For Sociology: Renewal and Critique in Sociology Today* (London: Allen Lane, 1973), pp. 87–8.
3. Michael Phillipson, Chapter 5 in Paul Filmer, Michael Phillipson, David Silverman and David Walsh, *New Directions in Sociological Theory* (London: Collier-Macmillan, 1972), p. 107.
4. Ibid.
5. Ralf Dahrendorf, *Society and Democracy in Germany* (London: Weidenfeld and Nicolson, 1968), p. 99.
6. For a statement of this case, see George A. Lundberg, *Can Science Save Us?* (New York: David McKay, 2nd edition, 1961), Ch. 2.
7. Max Weber, 'Science as a Vocation', in H. H. Gerth and C. Wright Mills (eds.), *From Max Weber: Essays in Sociology* (London: Routledge and Kegan Paul, 1948), pp. 145–6.
8. For example, G. Sartori, 'The Sociology of Parties', in O. Stammer (ed.), *Party Systems, Party Organisations and the Politics of New Masses* (Berlin: Free University, 1968).
9. Paul Halmos, *The Personal Service Society* (London: Constable, 1970), pp. 65–91.

10. Ralf Dahrendorf, *Essays in the Theory of Society* (London: Routledge and Kegan Paul, 1968), p. 17.
11. T. S. Simey, *Social Science and Social Purpose* (London: Constable, 1968), p. 188.
12. Ibid., Ch. 5.
13. Stanley Cohen (ed.), *Images of Deviance* (Harmondsworth: Penguin, 1971), Editor's introduction, pp. 22–3.
14. Paul Walton, 'The Case of the Weathermen', in Ian Taylor and Laurie Taylor (eds.), *Politics and Deviance* (Harmondsworth: Penguin, 1973), pp. 163–4.
15. Ibid., pp. 165–6.
16. Alvin Gouldner, *The Coming Crisis in Western Sociology* (London: Heinemann, 1971), p. 498.

Index

academic life, academics:
alienation of, 112
demands of social system in, 16
individual's definition of the
situation in, 55–6, 67
interpretation of social norms in,
51–2
public image of, 31
role-conflict of professor, 94
role playing, 89
see also school
alienation, 35, 102, 138, 167, 172
and deviance, 105–6, 107, 127–31
and false consciousness, 155–6
and power, 133
and social roles, 106–16
'alternative' or 'underground' press,
27–8
American society:
conformity in, 11
goal of material success and status
in, 126, 128
norms and social change in, 53
political alienation in, 107
power structure of, 146
role expectation in, 75–6, 77–8
The American Soldier (Stouffer), 73
Angry Brigade, 174
anomie, theory of, 49, 116–17, 126–7,
128
anticipatory socialisation, 73
appearance v. reality, notion of, 89,
90–1, 101–2
army:
marginality in, 73
NCOs' role conflict in, 93
soldiers' definition of situation in,
29–30
As You Like It, 100
authorities, 32, 65, 66, 176
authority, 76, 132, 135, 156

and ideology, 139–45
see also élites

Barchester Towers, 73–4
Berger, Peter, 95–6, 114
Blau, Peter, 133–4, 139
businessmen, business executives, 16,
27, 38
deviance of, 121
impression management of, 87
role conflict of, 94
role distance of, 99
role expectation of, 75–6
social status and, 151
Butler, David, 152–3

capitalism, 17
Marx's critique of, 108, 130–1, 138,
145, 147
Chapman, Dennis, 121–2, 123, 124
charismatic authority, 140–1
chess player, role embracement of,
98–9
child labour, 24
Christianity, 16, 37, 38, 44, 69
Cicourel, Aaron, 122
class consciousness, 152–3, 154, 168
see also false consciousness; social
classes
clergyman, 16
role distance of, 96
social status of, 150, 151
Coates, Ken, 71
Cohen, Stanley, 174
common-sense theories, 10, 28, 36, 47
objectivity and, 164–5, 175–6, 177
communication out of character,
89–90, 96
community power studies, 134–5
comparative reference groups, 68–70,
71

186

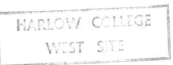